The Plug

PURPOSEFUL LIVING UNTO GOD

Spring Taft

Copyright © 2019 by Spring Taft

All rights reserved. No part of this publication may be reproduced by any means, graphics, electronic, or mechanical, including photocopying, recording, taping, or by any information storage retrieval system without the written permission of the publisher except in the case of brief quotations embodied in critical articles and reviews.

Spring Taft/Rejoice Essential Publishing
PO BOX 512
Effingham, SC 29541

www.republishing.org

Unless otherwise indicated, scripture is taken from the King James Version.

Scripture quotation marked (NIV) taken from the Holy Bible, New International Version®, NIV®. Copyright © 1973, 1978, 1984, 2011 by Biblica, Inc.™ Used by permission of Zondervan. All rights reserved worldwide. www.zondervan.com

The Plug/ Spring Taft

ISBN-10: 1-946756-56-3
ISBN-13: 978-1-946756-56-5
Library of Congress Control Number: 2019907987

Dedication

"This book is dedicated to all the youth, and young adults: domestic and abroad."

Rev. Levi Gay Grandfather (Mentor)

Dream Inspired Live Inspired***Be Inspired***

*** Let God be your PLUG***

#TeamYI4R

Table of Content

INTRODUCTION..1

CHAPTER ONE: Tragedy................3

CHAPTER TWO: Shock..................17

CHAPTER THREE: Trauma...............32

CHAPTER FOUR: Disconnect..........60

CHAPTER FIVE: Static..................67

CHAPTER SIX: New Sound.........76

CHAPTER SEVEN: Melody...............83

CHAPTER EIGHT: Connection.........90

CONCLUSION...106

ABOUT THE AUTHOR.... 121

Introduction

I can't sleep because it seems as if the noise of life has gotten so loud. I can hardly hear my thoughts and cries out loud. I feel like I'm racing fast. I prayed to God that I could pass this class. The class is called life, and unfortunately, I'm failing because I keep derailing my dreams, my hopes, my visions, but, ultimately, my purpose. I'm overwhelmed, overworked, and tired. My life is so loud that I can barely hear it. It feels like I'm stuck in the midst of a crowd. And, I'm screaming and no one can hear my sound. I need time so I can go, stretch out, and get inspired. On the altar is where I lay my burdens when I'm tired. My life is so loud that I can barely hear it, like it's a crowd. My godmother always told me even as a child, "Take everything to God in prayer." Well, I'm asking you, God, to silence the noise and turn up the volume of Your voice because I need You like never before. This man won't leave me alone. My mom barely knows I exist. What if I just disappeared? Sometimes I wish I didn't exist. It all seems like an awful, lousy dream. One I can't wake up out of; that's scary from scene to scene. I want the noise to stop, and Your voice to be loud and clear. I want to release my own sound; something that rings clear for all to hear. For the joy of the Lord is my strength and refuge. Whom shall I fear? For when my mother and father forsake me, God shall take me up. Please remember me, Lord. I don't want to give up.

Trust in the LORD with all your heart and lean not on your own understanding. In all your ways submit to him, and he will make your paths straight. —Proverbs 3:5-6

CHAPTER ONE

Tragedy

A tragedy is described as a disastrous event, calamity, misfortune, or a serious drama typically depicting a significant conflict or situation. Let's say in this portion of my life, sorrow was my best friend, and I just learned to accept her tragedy.

We're going to start with my senior year of High School, but before we begin there, I am going to give you some history on a girl named Spring. There were a lot of ups and downs in my life, but God saw me through it all. My entire life, growing up, I was called something other than my name like stupid, fat, special, retard, or reject. Although I was given a unique name, people never called me by it. It was always something negative or derogatory to tear me down, so it stuck with me, all my life. Those were the names I answered to.

Growing up was anything from perfect. My life, honestly, was a circus of constant chaos that never seemed to die down but only multiply the more I stayed around. Growing up, I didn't have much. I watched my mom struggle with life. As I grew up, I noticed certain things. I had seen certain things, so by the time I made it to High School, I was practically a full-fledged adult, or so I thought. It was my freshman year of High School. I was so excited because I got accepted into an academically gifted High School. It was about an hour away from my house which meant I would have to wake up early to attend. At this time, my mom had gotten behind on bills. We were running extension cords from our neighbor's home to our home. I felt so bad for my little brother and I because of what we had to deal with: this lousy hand we were dealt called "Life."

The Plug   5

I wanted to help, but I also wanted to eat. So, I used my body to get the things I needed. I know what you're saying. How could you? Well, honestly, how could I not at the time is what I thought. It was just one person. We had an agreement. I was ashamed, but I didn't have a want. I knew who God was. Well, He knew me, but we were not well acquainted at this time.

Now, let's fast forward to my Senior year of High School. "Listen Spring. You're going to have to pull your weight around here. I need you to go to Walmart and fill out an application. You are the only one eligible to work in the household." "Ok, Ma," was my reply. I didn't have much to say. I have always been a helper so helping my family seemed like a no-brainer. It was just balancing everything in my Senior year of High School and my honors' classes. But I knew it would work for me, it always does. That Friday, I got a call from my Aunt, who was the store manager of Walmart. She told me I was hired. I was thrilled and excited to have my first job. I adjusted my schedule, so I got out of school at noon instead of 2:30 pm. I quickly called my godmother, "MA! I got my schedule worked out." She said, "Baby, focus on school. If you can get yourself to work, I can pick you up every night." I said, "That is a plan." There was so much going on in my life. "I am a Senior. I am a young adult. I am on my way to college, or so I thought." I would not get home from my job till after midnight. All I knew was that I had to sustain my family, but I was so tired and worn out. I still had to study, do my term papers, and projects.

It was payday! I was too excited, but before my excitement could transfer into MONEY MOVES, my mom called me. "Spring, please come straight home with your paycheck." "But mom I need..." "Come HOME!" So as my mom requested, I went home. I remember my pastor preaching for a few weeks on tithes and offering. Tithes should be 10% of your earnings, and your offering should be a love token to God. So, I was so excited to pay tithes for the first time. Not only was I a Senior in High School, I also formed a praise dance group in the church, and I sang in the choir. I was the first young person in my church to catch the Holy Ghost. Finally, I made it home. My mom said, "This is what you have left from your check aside from the bills." I looked and said, "It's just enough to pay my tithes." I felt defeated and confused. But I said I was going to pay my tithes, so that's what I did. My godmother picked me up from work. We had one of our late-night chats about life my future and being a good steward over my finances. I had several late-night conversations with my godmother at the time.

The conversation I constantly replayed in my mind was when I told her that I felt like my life had no meaning, and I didn't want to live anymore. I told her they were just thoughts, but my home life was HELL. I was walking as an adult but still being a child. She said, "Baby! That's a spirit. You must ask God every day to renew your mind and cast your cares on Him because He cares for you." She made me make a promise to her that if I ever felt like the waves were coming in too strong and they would take me out in the current to let her know. She wept as she repeated this to me. I replied, "MA! I promise. I'm ok."

School was going great! As I walked into the main office to get a copy of my transcript, I looked down. I noticed a flyer for Debutante Ball for participants ages 6-19. I immediately texted my godmother and asked if I could be a part of this. She said, "I think it would be great for you to learn etiquette." I enrolled in Colors of World Inc. Debutante Ball. I had rehearsal every Saturday. I had to learn to dance, Waltz to be exact, but I felt like a princess. But I would soon be running into some royal problems. My mom took me to the best dressmaker in town. She let me pick out the perfect dress. The women at the shop said every few weeks I would have to come in and get fitted for the dress and put down a deposit.

So immensely, my mom sat me down. We strategically came up with a budget that would allow me to pay my dress off, pay my tithes, and still have a little savings leftover. My godmother suggested at the time that I should not buy lunch at school and work anymore. She told me to pack my lunch and to conserve my spending. That night, I went to work. I was so excited. I bought myself a case of water, some crackers, chips, and little things that I could bring to school and work so I did not have to spend unnecessary money on food. When my godmother dropped me off, she said, "Spring, put those things in your room so, they don't go fast." As I'm entering the house, it's already late, I must pass my mom's room to get to the back of the house where my room was. As I was in my room, I aligned the stuff I brought against my wall. "Perfect," I said. I felt like I was doing something. Small joys bring me so much happiness. There was a knock at my door. "Yea, who is it?" "It's me, Spring!" My mother was at my bedroom door. When I got up to answer it, I could tell by her demeanor that it wasn't going to be a good conversation. I said, "Yes!" Her response was, "What did you just bring into this house?" I replied, "Some snacks, so I can stop spending money at school and work on food."

My mother's rebuttal was, "Well put the things in the kitchen, so we can all get some of it." I replied, "No. These things are for me. I don't have money to buy food, and I work three to midnight every day. I need to watch how I spend my money." My mother began to snatch up the things in my room and drag them to the kitchen. At that point, I started to get mad. I thought, "Jesus, I have two term papers to write, and I don't have time. You know me, Lord. Help me before I SNAP!" My mom continued yelling at me saying that I wasn't this and I wasn't that. I was not going to be anything. At that moment, I felt a heat wave cross over my body and out of my mouth came the true contents of my heart. I said, "I'm tired of this! I'm tired of you! I'm doing the best that I can as a kid trying to enjoy my last year in High School. What more do you want from me?" My mother proceeded to yell, "You think you're going to college with what money? Why can't you share it with your family? You don't do anything for us."

I SNAPPED again! But by this time, she had called my older sister and brother. So, it went from control in the house of disagreement to us yelling on the front porch. My sister Ra'shae told us to calm down. I was so full of anger I couldn't calm myself down. I said, "I've been there when I was the only one who wanted you to get help. For you to stop doing drugs." So, my sister looked at me and said, "Don't spread lies." I said, "It was the truth." I remember walking back into the house to grab my book bag and phone. I planned to run away that night and never return. I was so hurt and broken from the situation. I thought no one cared and God had left me. I walked off.

My sister and brother had gone into the house to speak with my mom. It was after 1:30 am.

As I walked down the street, I saw the Bishop of "Total Praise House of Worship" standing outside. He looked at me. He didn't say a word, but I knew he was praying for me. I couldn't leave my street. I didn't live in the best neighborhood, so it was not safe for me to be outside. I waited for my sister and brother to leave. Then, I went back inside. When I went inside, all my stuff that was pulled in the kitchen was at my bedroom door. I kicked it all in my room and cried. I prayed myself to sleep that night. I remember asking God why the simplest things in my life must be so complicated.

My alarm sounded at 6 am. It was not something that I wanted to hear that morning after getting into a big fight with my mom the previous night. I had to be at my honors' class at the community college to turn in the outline for my term paper. Then, I had college prep moreover mentoring. Finally, I was done with my school day, so I went to work. My godmother called me and stated that I needed a date for my Debutante

Ball. I said, "I think I have someone in mind." I was going to ask Antwon from the church. My godmother stated that it would be a great idea. She reached out to Antwon's mother to fill her in the details and gauge whether he was going to be interested.

The next day was the rehearsal. My godmother brought me and Antwon to my rehearsal. After rehearsal, there was no hanging out for me because I had to go straight to work. "Girl come on. Why are you dragging? I'm the one who is pregnant," were the words that came out my best friend Britney's mouth. As we walked to school, Brit, asked, "Spring, where do you see yourself in five years?" I said, "Brit, a college graduate on my way to becoming a Corporate Attorney, NOT being here!" Brit said, "That's my girl. I want to be a great mom and finish college so I can become a Registered Nurse. I want to provide for my child, so he or she can be afforded the things I couldn't in my life." I said, "Britt, you're going to make it. You and my godchild have me. I won't leave you."

Finally, we made it to school. The school week went on like every other school week. I couldn't wait till church on Sunday. I had gotten paid, and I had my tithes. But this Sunday was different. My Pastor talked about Super Seed Sunday which would happen in a few weeks. Pastor Marcus stated that each person, including the kids, should get a seed in their hand to come around and drop in the basket. Pastor Marcus said, "Whether it's 1 dollar or 20 dollars, we are going to rejoice for every gift and celebrate each person." Pastor Marcus told everyone to pray to God, and whatever number God gives you to sow on top of your tithes, that's what you give. He also went on to say when you drop your money in the baskets, to ask God for something major.

So, leaving the church, I told my mom what God had dropped in my spirit. I said, "God said 120 dollars above my tithes." My godmother, Regina, said, "That's going to take you being frugal over the next few weeks." I said, "I can do this!" Back at school, it was a week before Thanksgiving which is my favorite Holiday because of my best friend Brit's birthday. As I'm walking down the hallway in school, I see Britt in between my class. I go up to her. "Hey, girlie. You don't look so good." She states she had a major migraine. I know what those feel like since I suffer with them as well. I said, "Well, you can't take regular medicine. Let's take a walk next door to the hospital." So, me, Britt, and her sister Camilla, walked over to the hospital. At this point, I called out of work because they hadn't seen Britt yet. The doctors finally came and said, "Ms. Parker, your blood is a little low and you're pregnant. So, we are going to keep you overnight." I said, "Britt, I can stay with you." She said, "No." But she needed some things from home which was her Aeropostale hoodie and her Teddy bear. I said, "Ok. I'll bring it up to you.

For a week, Camilla and I went back and forth to the hospital. Ring. "Hello." "Hey, Britt. Happy Birthday." "Thank you, thank you! Now come and rescue me. Bring me some food." I told Britt what my grandmother had cooked and that I was packing her plate at that moment. She told me to save it and bring it to her Monday. I said, "You Got it! How's baby boy cooking?" She said, "Just fine." I spoke with Britt all weekend long.

That Sunday was Super Seed Sunday. I had my Tithes, offering, and Super Seed." Pastor

Marcus preached an amazing message entitled "Maximizing Your Abilities in God." He said that everything we do should be done in excellence as if you're doing it unto God. Of course, I praised and worshiped God because that was my heart's desire: to live a life that's pleasing unto God. Well, it was offering time in the house, and Pastor Marcus made us recite a faith confession over our finances. The congregation repeated,

"Our Father, I thank and praise You now for Your Word and Your provision. Thank You, God, for providing seed for me to sow at this time. I am a cheerful and excited giver. I know that when I give, it shall be given back to me in good measure, pressed down, shaken together, and running over. I sow in good soil which is my church, my Pastor, and the kingdom of God. Thank You, God, that the devil is rebuked for my sake. Blessings pursue me and overtake me every day of my life. Your Word declares that if I serve and obey, I will spend my days in prosperity and my years in pleasure. I AM DEBT FREE! NEW GREATER MISSION BAPTIST CHURCH IS DEBT FREE! Thank You, God, for setting up people now who somehow someway will use their power, ability, and influence on my behalf. I set and position myself to receive what I have spoken. In Jesus' name Amen. Amen. and Amen."

Three men were standing in each aisle with a basket and microphone. The Pastor had a bell he rang every time someone gave. Now, remember I said the Pastor said when you drop the money in the basket request something from God, that you want. So, it was my turn, and I dropped my money in the basket. I silently prayed and asked God if I could be accepted into college. I prayed that it would be fully or close as possible to a full ride. As the money dropped in the basket, the Pastor and other members rang the bells. I was the last one, so they tallied everything together. God worked it out because we exceeded our goal. When church was over, as usual, I had to go to work. I couldn't wait to get to school that Monday so I could tell Britt and everyone what I did.

The Lord is nigh to them that are of a broken heart; and saveth such as be of a contrite spirit.— Psalms 34:18

CHAPTER TWO

Shock

TO BE IN SHOCK is defined as a sudden upsetting or surprising event or experience. Also, it is a violent shaking movement caused by an impact, explosion, or tremor. My life was all these things in that season, and so much more. Beep.. Beep ! My phone alarm went off at 6:15 am. I was sluggish but moving because I was excited to see Britt that day. As I entered the school, I could hear the security guards calling my name over the radios as I walked in. I walked up to get searched with a wand then walked through the metal detectors. They immediately escorted me to the guidance counselor office. I kept asking, "What did I do wrong?" He then just kept saying, "They need to see you." When I walked in, Ms. Harold was standing there with a saddened look on her face. So, I thought I was getting suspended or kicked out my honors' class. So, I started pleading to do better by telling her, "It's just that I've been working a lot." She stopped me and said, "No. That's not it." She asked, "When was the last time you spoke with Brittany?" I said, "Yesterday. I am going to visit her after school." Ms. Harold said, "Spring, I regret to inform you, but Britt has passed away."

I immediately said, "You're lying!" I picked up her phone on her desk and called Brit's phone. I got no answer. I walked out of school because the hospital was right next door. I ran in the inside. I asked the lady at the front desk if I could see my sister. She said, "What's her name?" I said, "Brittney Parker." Ten minutes later a person from the mortuary came up to tell me she passed, and they just brought her downstairs. I ran out

The Plug 19

of the hospital. The man asked if I needed to talk to anyone.

I just kept running. Tears filled my eyes so much, it was hard to see. I ran to my best friend's house. Her mom opened the door, but she didn't say anything. She just embraced me and cried. Over the next few days, I didn't attend school because I was so hurt. I couldn't cope with her not being there in my classes with me. It was finally the day of her funeral. I asked my godmother to come with me. She said she would, but she had a long talk with me before we got there. She said, "You and your friends lost someone special. I can't imagine how you feel. But you, Spring, must be an anchor for your friends and a beacon of hope. You can't walk up, say your last goodbyes, and fall apart." I said, "I won't," which was the hardest promise I had to make and keep to my godmother. When we arrived at the church, her mom and her sister asked me to walk in with them. So, I did. As I'm walking down the long middle aisle of this church, I felt like my legs were buckling like I was walking on stilts. But I stayed strong.

Towards the end of the service, the officiant asked if there were last remarks, and this would be the last time to see her and say goodbye. So, my other four friends and I got up. We said goodbye together. We interlocked our arms. I stood in the middle, and everyone else was on the outside. As we walked together, I remembered the words my mom said to me about being the anchor. I stayed strong. I didn't lose hope because I am a believer in Christ. I knew that I would see her again. The upcoming next few days, I knew I had to attend school because it was midterms. Although I missed my friend deeply, I still needed to finish out the school year. I went back to school and to work. I tried to continue my same schedule. On Saturday, I had a Debutante rehearsal. Afterward, I had to go to work. I was excited about church on Sunday.

I had been feeling so heavy and burdened down. I needed a release. So, what better way than to give God, true praise and worship. It's in these moments that I release so much stress and I went to another level in my faith. I pushed past pain. I went into praise and worship that was so authentic. After an incredible weekend of laying

The Plug

at God's feet, I received a letter in the mail for a college interview for my top choice school. I immediately called my god mom and asked her if she could call arrange a date for me to have a tour and interview.

Over the next few days, I was anxiously waiting to hear when I would go to this school. My godmother called me with excitement in her voice. "Do you have to work on Friday." I said, "Umm, I think so." "Can you switch your schedule to go to your college interview?" I said, "Yes, I'll call them now and let them know I will not be at work." On Friday, my mom picked me up from school at noon, and we went to my college interview. I dressed business casual, as I've never been on that type of interview before. When we arrived at the campus, the admissions representative immediately took us on a campus tour of the residence halls. I was very impressed at how modern and distinguished it looked. Then we walked back on the main campus, and we had an interview for about 30 minutes. When we left, my godmother told me, "This is the school for you. How do you feel about it?" I said, "How do you know I'll get accepted?" She said, "You will," and smiled. I always admired my godmother's faith. If she believed it and prayed, she knew it would happen.

On watch night service, I was happy to go to church. My godmother, Regina, told me that she would pick me up at 10 pm. Of course, I was the only one in my household getting ready to bring in the New Year with God. No worries. I still laid my family at God's feet. I prayed for Him to heal, set them free, and deliver them. So, while I was getting dressed, I noticed my stepdad, Kyle, was home. As usual, he was drunk. He always had a way of making me uncomfortable when he was intoxicated. So, on this night, he decided to make a pass at me by hinting towards something inappropriate. I immediately called my godmother and asked, "How far are you from my house? He's here. He is drunk, making passes and gestures at me." She said, "Step out on the porch. I'll talk to you till I get there. I'm five minutes away." My godmother finally pulled up, and I couldn't be happier.

I was ready to get into God's presence, and that is precisely what I did. I worshiped for the whole night. I needed to shed some things. I was so glad I did. A few weeks went by, and I received a big, white envelope in the mail. I promptly called my godmother and told her I was nervous about opening it. She said, "Bring it to Youth BIBLE Study tonight." So, I packed up my stuff and headed out the door. While being in youth BIBLE Study, all I thought about was the envelope. It bothered me so bad that I got up. I walked out and went outside to read it in private. The letter read, "Congratulations Spring Taft on being accepted to Post University and being a part of the graduating class of 2012." I just held the letter in shock. I couldn't believe it! Behind my offer letter was my award letter. My college tuition was partially paid for, all except for 1000 dollars.

I started jumping and shouting. One of the youth advisors walked outside and asked, "Is everything ok?" I said, "Yes, I'm fine." She said, "Well, you're missing a good lesson. Let's get inside." I wanted to tell my youth advisor the good news, but I wanted to show my godmother first. When church was over, I rode with my godmother to drop the other youth off at home. While she was on the way to drop me off, I said, "Here is the letter. I opened it." She asked, "So, what does it say?" I said, "Read it." As she read the letter, she went up into a praise. She pulled over the church van and started doing laps around it, saying "Thank you, JESUS!" She had not gotten to the award letter, so I said, "Look. Keep reading." She went and evoked God's presence outside by worshiping Him. It was like she requested something from Him for me and He answered her for me. So, she had finally calmed down enough to drive us home, but she was still worshiping God.

The next upcoming week was crucial because I was finally doing my last fitting for my Debutante Ball. My second to last rehearsal was that Saturday. The week progressed like any other week, until Friday. It seemed like anything that could go wrong was going wrong. So, my godmother told me to call her on her lunch break. She needed to talk to me about something. I said, "Ok." So, I called her, and she said, "Spring, I am having trouble with finding someone to step in to play the role of your dad." I became dismayed because my maternal parents and I have an unhealthy relationship. On the one day that I don't need my dysfunctional upbringing to show, it does. So, I hung up in a very agitated tone. I thought, "Oh well, I won't do it. It's canceled!" This is how I dealt with my pain and discomfort. If I couldn't cope, I just shut down to save myself from falling apart.

So that afternoon, I went over to the dress shop. I advised the women that I was there for my fitting. She looked a little nervous and hesitant. I asked, "Is everything alright?" She said, "Don't be mad, but a bride came in and fell in love with your Princess Ball gown." I said, "Ok, where is it?" She said, "I sold it." I felt my blood pressure boil over, but this time I just called my mom. In a panic, I yelled, "She sold my dress! WHAT'S is going on?" After the dressmaker spoke with my mom, she apologized and said she has another dress I would probably like. I said, "No, I'm ok. I want all my money back for the dress and the alterations. I'm done." So, my godmother made it happen, but I still felt very discouraged because I didn't have parents to walk me into my ball. Because my dress was resold, I would not attend my ball. That night I went to work, and when I got off, my godmother had a long talk with me.

She could see my continence had changed and I had become saddened over the whole situation. I started to cry and asked my god mom, "Why?" "How come I can't have normal parents?" I began to get angry, and my mom told me Psalms 27:10.

When my father and my mother forsake me, then the LORD will take me up.— Psalms 27:10

She said, "God has a wonderful adoption agency. It's better than anything you have ever seen. He will lead people in your life to help protect you and guide you towards His purpose for you. I looked up at her and said, "Ok." I honestly felt better knowing that God would take care of me. Still, I decided to not participate because my dress was not there, and the replacement wasn't for me. My godmother gave me the money for everything. I said, "Let's put half up now for when I go away to college." She said, "Ok." I got my hair done that weekend then went and just got pampered. Sometimes you need to do that for yourself every now and again. I had been working so hard. I was feeling drained and waiting for the summer to come so I could finally take a break and chill because working full-time and going to school is a lot. I was doing it to change my situation and circumstances. About three weeks before prom, I decided that I did not want to go even though I bought my ticket already. I did not have a chance to get the dress I wanted made. My pockets were extremely low. One week before my prom, my godmother calls me and says, "Come over to Nana's house." I asked, "Why? What's up?" My godmother said, "Just come." I showed up, and my godmother had brought me the most elegant prom dress ever. It was sky blue with a built-in blinged out belt. I thanked her so much. She said, "Spring, you deserve to go to your prom." Now that happened the Friday before my prom. I went to church that Sunday and broke through the presence of God by giving Him true worship and praise because even when I didn't have a way, He made the way for me.

Many times, on our faith journey, we become dismayed at how the situation looks. But unfortunately, we are only seeing a small picture of a grand picture that God is creating. Don't get caught up in the 'what it looks like' at first. So that Monday, I had to call my hair stylist to see if she had any openings early Friday morning. I called. She did have an opening at 11 am. I said that was fine. Then, I had to figure out my shoes. Guess what? God provided that too. My godmother brought me some shiny silver nine west pump sandals, but God didn't stop there. I was able to get my makeup professionally done at MAC and get some touch-up products. Now I was spinning my wheels on how I was going to get there being that my prom was 30 minutes away. Tell me why God had that covered too!

My godmother pulled up to my grandmother GG's house in a new Chrysler. It was silver and shining like my shoes. On Friday it was prom day! I got dressed at my grandmother GG's house. Everyone was taking pictures of me. I felt like a celebrity because everyone was helping me get dressed by fixing this and adjusting that. I was ready to go. My godmother wanted to take pictures with my siblings and me. As I was walking down the stairs, my mom slid some money in my hand. I was shocked that she did that. So, I said, "No, I have some money." She said, "No, take it." That little small measurement of hope is what I held on to the whole night because a few weeks earlier, I felt like I was an abandoned child. It felt nice to know and see my mom caring about me.

So, my godmother got me a luxury rental, and she was my chauffeur to get me to my prom. I was so excited sitting in the backseat because two weeks prior, I would have never thought this would be happening. But isn't that just like God? When we don't see a way, and we look at the picture as defeat, He sees us as victorious. God was working in the background on my behalf. I finally made it to prom, and I had a great time. It felt like I finally made it to a point where I could let my hair down. My breakthrough had come. So as a senior, I was finally feeling the joy and the excitement of a new chapter happening in my life.

Two weeks before graduation, we were having rehearsals, and we got to leave school early. But on this particular day, we had an award ceremony. I wasn't going to go because I didn't think I was going to get any awards. The award ceremony started. Guess whose name they called five times? Mines! I was so excited and shocked because I had not applied for any of these awards nor was I in expectation of receiving any. But I was so glad to see how God worked it out for my good. Through all the tired nights of no sleep and the pain of feeling like I couldn't do it, God rewarded me because of my faithfulness.

I was so excited on my graduation day. I woke up early that morning, fixed my hair, and showed up at the arena early. When they called my name, I was super excited. All I could hear was people SCREAMING my name, "Spring!" I turned around and saw my whole family there in support of me. Even my biological father was in attendance. I was so shocked and in awe of how God had worked everything out for my good. The pain of my heartache seemed so worth it for this one moment. My principal handed me my diploma. I smiled and walked off stage. A few weeks before I was to leave to go away to college, I was working hard as I could to save money so when I went away, I would have plenty.

It was move-in day for all the freshmen. I woke up that morning and organized my things several times to make sure I did not forget anything. My godmother pulled up in the U-Haul. I was already dragging my stuff to the porch. It took all of 30 minutes to pack everything into the truck. Before we left the house, we said a prayer for God to bless me while I was in school and for me to remember the founding principles that were instilled into me. When the prayer was done, I tried to call everyone in my immediate family to see if they wanted to see me off to college. I got no answers or a lot of no's. It discouraged my spirit, but I heard the Lord say, "It's working for your good," and I held on to that word.

Ask of me, and I shall give thee the heathen for thine inheritance, and the uttermost parts of the earth for thy possession.— Psalms 2:8

CHAPTER THREE

Trauma

TO BE IN TRAUMA is to have a deeply distressing or disturbing experience.

Well, let's say in this season of my life, it was a 911 emergency. I needed God like 'now.' LIKE RIGHT NOW! You know what? Even though I was in my wilderness season, I felt like God Himself had deserted me. I still had to stay connected to God regardless of my current state. Ring. Beep. Ring. "Hello." "Spring! Come home!

Terrance has been shot!" I looked at my phone, and it was 2 am. I said, "Can you come to get me?" I went into deep prayer. The phone call I had gotten was about my favorite cousin who had been shot, and it was not looking good. When I got home, I immediately wanted to go to the hospital. When I got there, I prayed over him and with my family. I prayed that God would spare his life. I stayed at his bedside for two weeks praying and crying with my family during the last semester of my senior year. I couldn't focus. I just wanted God to hear my prayer and save him. But it was not according to God's will. My cousin took his last breaths as I stood at his bedside with my family on February 28, 2012. He was laid to rest on March 8, 2012.

That was a hard place and time for me because I felt that God liked to see me in pain and hurting. I felt like God could have saved my cousin, but He didn't. It hurt so bad. I tried to keep things together when I was in a place of questioning and doubting my faith. I had to just push aside how I felt and help my family and plan my cousin's funeral. Creating his slide show and information was hard because I was in a place of grief. It was hard for me to see God through the fog of my pain. After the services, I heard the Lord tell me to do something I had never done before. He told me to go be with my cousin's mom in her time of grief to deal with the transition. I asked her and because we already had such a great relationship, she was very understanding of me. I was going to be moving out of state. I transferred my college classes online because of the situation which meant I would not finish school until the winter of that year. I got everything switched and moved out of college. Down south I went. I witnessed to my cousin every day and let her know it was ok to feel the way she was feeling. The place of pain that she felt would, in time, be filled with an abundance of joy. But as I told her this, I believed it for her, but not for myself. I stayed with my cousin for a total of seven months. Seven being the month of completion. I finished the task God had asked me to do.

When I returned home, I realized that I did not have a home to return to. When I docked back into Connecticut, I called my birth mother, Samantha. I asked her if I could come over, shower, and stay with her for a while. She told me,

The Plug 35

"NO!" I wasn't welcomed at her home. I wept in deep despair because at that point, I was homeless. So, what was I to do now? I called a guy friend who I had been dating before I left home. I asked if he would help me. I was not looking for anything from this individual, but it was inevitable. I felt like I had no job, no money, and nowhere to go. So, this was as good as it gets for me.

It was now September. The winter before I completed college, I found a decent corporate job. But because I never wanted to be broke, I picked up another job at Dunkin Donuts part-time. So I was working during the day, not driving, and working overnight. Things were finally looking up for me. I was blessed with my own place. It was only a few months into having my own place, and I love it! I felt like God was showering His blessing on me and I was excited.

As I approached my one year anniversary at my job, they told me and a few of my colleagues they were downsizing the company, and our department will be cut. "I regretfully hate to inform you, Spring, but you and your department's last day is this Friday." I stood there in shock.

I walked out of the HR (Human Resources) meeting and just left work. As I walked away, I thought, "What am I going to do? I cannot afford my apartment with my part-time job." So, I became depressed and while I boarded the bus, the spirit of suicide fell on me heavily so much that I was inconsolable. I went on my Facebook and posted, "I apologize to my parents for being such a constant failure and for coming into this world when they both were not ready." I was still on the bus, so I took the bus to the river dockside where the ferries dock in at. I cried and apologized to God for always having such bad luck. I made one last post to my Facebook. It said, "Goodbye."

When I get to the dock, I threw my purse and jacket in the water. Before I climbed over the dock fence, I asked this woman one question. "What makes life worth living?" She looked down at her son and said, "Him."

I said, "Nah, I don't have one of those!" As I am about to climb over the fence and jump, my phone rings. I saw that my godfather had called me several times. But I had not noticed because I was in such a daze. I answered as I sat on the edge. He

The Plug 37

says, "Spring, precious woman of God. My child, talk to me!" I said, "Dad! This is just a buildup of years of hurt and pain. I lost my job. I'm going to be homeless. My life's not fair. I can't take it anymore!" He said, "Pray with me, Spring!" During his praying, my phone died on him. So, now I am sitting on the edge of the dock crying and READY to END my LIFE. At that moment, God spoke to me and clearly said, "Trust Me one more time." It was the beginning of the summer currently, and the sun was shining. Then it started to rain on me as I climbed off the ledge. I just sat there in the rain and just cried out to God.

I ended up moving out of my place and going to my aunt's house temporarily. She said she would talk to my mom the next day with me. We went together, and she asked my mother, Samantha, to take me in until I got back up on my feet. My mother replied and said something I wasn't expecting to hear. She said she has friends and knew some men. She was hinting to something I couldn't understand. Honestly, I didn't want to understand at that time. My aunt said, "It's your daughter." She said, "When I needed her, she wasn't there for me." I was so angry and hurt. I yelled at my mother Samantha and walked out. I told my aunt, "Don't beg her to do anything for me. I'm good." Now, because of what my mom had said, I wanted to go back to that riverside. But I was holding on to the promise that God had given me, "Trust Him one more time."

From my aunt's house, I went to stay with a distant cousin. I went from having my own everything to being a stranger in someone else's home in a blink of an eye. With all the stress that I was under, my epilepsy was out of control. I would be walking, then blackout, have a seizure, and wake up in the hospital. Not knowing how I got there, I just felt like I was tired and defeated. I couldn't see my way out, but I continued to attend church. I even served in the church. I joined the praise team and the intercessors team. I participated in shut-in services. I was trying to stay close to God because I felt like if I walked away, I would DIE.

One of the members of the church took a liking to me. She saw me as her daughter. She called me that evening and said God said for her to help me. She asked, "Would you like to stay with me? I own a two-family home. My husband, myself, and

The Plug　　　　　　　　　　　　39

smaller kids live on one side. My other daughters live on the other side. They are looking for a roommate." I stalled for a month because to be quite honest. I heard God's answer when she first asked me. It was a 'no' and I didn't understand why, but I would soon find out. So, I told her yes. My decision was solely based off my emotions and thought process Mrs. Bryant said she would pick me up from the bus station once I was in town. So, as I was riding the bus to Mrs. Bryant's house, the Spirit of the Lord fell on me heavy. God began to pour into me by letting me know who I was and the very gifts and talents He has placed in me. I was inconsolable. I cried on the whole bus ride to my new destination.

I arrived at the bus terminal, and Mrs. Bryant was there waiting. When I arrived at the house, she immediately took me up to my room. It was big and massive. I had a double walk-in closet. Plus, I had my own bathroom. I just began to cry and thank God for this blessing and open door. The family accepted me as their own. It felt good. I felt like my life had a meaning and that I mattered. That desire for a close family situation that I always longed for as a child, I finally felt like it had shown up. We worshiped together and ate together. We were the ideal family picture, or so I thought. Things went well for a long time with me living with the Bryant's.

Overtime, things started to take a turn for the worse when I started acknowledging Mr. Bryant as my god father. For the first time, I felt like I had the consistent father figure in my life. But his stepdaughters, my god sisters (Rachel and Marissa), felt otherwise. There was a normal start to a Sunday in the Bryant's household. Everyone was up and getting themselves prepared to attend Greater Worship Assembly where the Senior Pastor is Gloria Lockhart. We all piled up in the cars to drive five minutes away to church. I couldn't wait to go into God's house that morning as I was the Senior Sound Tech in the church. I was responsible for the sound in the church. To ensure God's message would come across clean, I took my position in the church serious. When church was over, we went home.

As all the girls went into our side of the house, Mr. Bryant came over and wanted to speak us. We all went into the living room. Of course, I already knew the topic of the discussion, but I was prepared as I had been doing my part. The conversation started with, "Rachel, when are you and Rissa, going to get a job?" Mr. Bryant highlighted that I was working and paying them as I was supposed to. I responded by saying, "Dad! I'm just not trying to be homeless." I don't know if it was my spirit, but when I said "dad," Rachel got very angry. She said, "Don't ever say that again!" I said, "Why not? It's a sign of respect." Rachel went to critical max. She ran in the kitchen and grabbed a butcher knife. She proceeded to say, "Don't say it again!" I was still trying to figure out why she was so mad as I have a large knife in my face. So, Mr. Bryant gets up and grabs Rachel and told her to calm down. At this moment, I was so caught off guard. I just left the house and took a walk. I wished I could say that this was the only encounter I had with the Bryant's, but it wasn't. I started to understand a lot about why God gave me a 'no.'

My next encounter with the Bryant's was major. The two oldest girls moved out. They didn't want to be in their parents' house. They wanted to move with their grandmother in Maryland. So now it's just me left in the house. I was confused as to what would happen with me as I would not be able to pay the mortgage on this side of the house on my one salary. I was stressed. That evening when I came in from work, Mrs. Bryant told me that I could stay on the other side. Even though her daughters had left, Mr. Bryant was shutting off the lights. So that meant I couldn't charge my phone for work. But I dealt with it for over five months. At the end of this period, the daughters had wanted to return. I was excited to have my sisters come back home. But I was a little scared because things between my god sisters and I had gotten so bad. It was like trusting the devil when you know eventually that he would hurt and kill you. So, they moved back in. Things were going great. I had gotten a great job at a Prestigious bank in the state where I lived which meant higher pay. I could save more so eventually I could move out, or so I believed.

I continued to attend church and was very active there. I worked in the church's media department and sang on the praise team. I was going to the church a couple of times a week to pray in the temple. The shepherd of the house had asked me to join the new minister's class. I had to buy books like "The Person and Works of the Holy Spirit," by R.A Torrey. After we had gotten through the book and lessons, the Pastor said it was time for us to do our initial sermons. We only had three weeks to prepare. I was nervous and scared. I was doing personal shut-ins at the church so that I could hear from God. I placed myself on a personal fast. I did not communicate with people unless it was necessary. I only wanted to hear from God.

A couple of days before I had to speak, God gave me my message entitled, "When It's Time To Go Into the Delivery Room," A.K.A. "MyLabor Pains We're Worth It." I was so excited about my message. I kept studying and reading. The night before I had to minister, I prayed to God. I asked Him to allow my family to come out in large numbers to support me and let them get saved. Well, it was finally the day. I was super nervous as I sat on the first row. As I turned around, I noticed my grandmother and her best friend were in attendance. As the worship leader called my name and introduced me, I walked up to the pulpit. I greeted my shepherd, members, saints, and friends. Then

I said a prayer that God would speak through me. The next 30 minutes were a blur. The Holy Ghost took over and lit the church on fire! While preaching, it was like God was showing me my life up until that point on a DVD display. The power, or the anointing, is something that can't be explained, only lived. That night, I gave birth to purpose. I stepped into a new dimension in God! The blessings started flowing from my obedience. I got the bank job!

Before I could get too happy, the Bryant's let me know that I had one problem which they pointed out to me. My new job was 25 minutes from where I currently lived. I immediately started to feel defeated. They said they would bring me back and forth to work, but I had to pay them 400 dollars a month to do so. I didn't drive so I took the deal. I know what you are saying, "How does this help you, Spring?" Well, I didn't want to pass up on this amazing opportunity, so this was the best deal I had at the time. The Bryant's also stated because I was making more money, they would be going up on my rent. I said sure to what Mr. Bryant had said, "950 for your room plus transportation." So, they essentially wanted

1450.00 from me. Plus, they also wanted the additional 450.00 a month because at that time I was only paying them 500. So, they wanted the difference for all those months I didn't pay 950. Thus, the first six months on my job, I just turned over my checks to them. The Bryant's even had a system. Before I went to work, they would take me to the bank and asked me to make a withdraw.

I was so depressed and overwhelmed. I wanted out of this situation because I could not see how I was going to make it. So, I did something that should never be done. But out of my desperation, I did not heed to God's warning before I came to the Bryant's house. Now, I wanted out of my desperate situation, so I told a lie. Now lying, in any instance, is totally wrong. But for me, I felt it was my only way out. I called the Bryant's, and I told them that my grandmother had passed away. I was going to come home and leave to go to my cousin's house to be with my family in my time of need. They felt bad and said they understood. I worked my normal scheduled shift. I had my friend Alexius bring me home. The plan was foolproof, or so I thought.

When I pulled up to the house that night, I felt like the air had changed. I felt this gut retching pain at the bottom of my stomach. Lexi said, "You want me to wait?" I looked around and said, "No, Just leave. It's going to be one of those nights." I did not know that I was speaking prophetically. As I entered my house, Mrs. Bryant, her husband, Mr. Bryant, my two god sisters, Raya and Rissa, were all there sitting and waiting for me. I said, "Hi," to everyone. I could feel the air in the room was thick. I could feel the continence of their spirits rushing up against me.

Mrs. Bryant said, "Is there anything that you would like to say to us?" I replied and said, "No." Mrs. Bryant began to tell me that she had spoken to my biological mom, Sam. She had reached out to someone that knew her to send condolence about my grandma. As she was speaking these words, I could feel my stomach sink lower and lower. Mrs. Bryant asked, "Is your grandmother DEAD?" I stayed quiet. Mrs. Bryant said, "Let's call your mom, Spring." The feeling in my stomach only worsen. Mrs. Bryant dialed my mother's number. She said, "Hello. Can I speak with Samantha?" My mother said, "This is she." She said, "Sam, is your mother ALIVE?" My mother said, "Yes. I'm sitting next to her right now. I don't know why my daughter would say something so awful about her grandmother." I just closed my eyes. Mrs. Bryant went on to say, "We don't want your daughter anymore." My mother, Samantha, replied that she didn't want me either and I wasn't welcomed in her home. Mrs. Bryant said, "What should we do with her?" My mother Samantha replied, "It's not my problem anymore," then dropped the CALL! Now I was standing in a room feeling like I was on trial. I did do the crime, but to me, it was for some justifiable reasons. So, Mrs. Bryant said, "It's blood in or out in this family. So how would you like your punishment? We can each cut you, or we can beat you down." I felt like I was being crucified. They spat at me. I got beat up for hours and couldn't fight back.

So finally, that part was over. The family said that they didn't want to look at me anymore and I could go to my room. While I was in my room, I cried hysterically. I just wanted to die because my real mom didn't want to save me. I thought maybe I wasn't worth being saved. So, I sat on my bed crying, praying to God, and asking Him to fix the situation. Suddenly, in rushes Raya and Rissa.

Raya had a sharp knife in her hand, and she is coming directly at me. I didn't touch her. I remember waving my hands as if I was in worship. Raya cuts her sister Rissa instead of me. So now, my two god sisters are arguing and fighting with each other. I'm just standing there in awe because I didn't touch either of them. Up the stairs, runs Mrs. Bryant. She is yelling at me. It's like she isn't even coherent. Mrs. Bryant ran back down the stairs and said, "I'm going to kill her tonight," but it was the way she said it. She scared my god sisters and me. Mrs Bryant let out a weird sound. I'll tell you what I heard in my spirit. I heard the demons coming out of her. They told me to go in my room, lock the door, and don't open it. Mrs. Bryant was back upstairs, and she was still trying to get in my room with a large steak knife. I pushed a dresser up against my door, and I just cried. I really felt like at that moment I could have died.

Mrs. Bryant was unable to get in my room, so she stabbed in the wall to bust through my room.

The Plug

It was way too much for me to handle, so I called my god father, John, who lived in California. He answered the phone and said, "Hi, Springy, are you ok?" I said, "No." I began to explain and tell him that she was trying to bust through my room. He said, "Baby girl, those are legions assigned to kill you. Call on JESUS! Now! Spring, out of your mouth!" So, I was now pressed up against my door, calling on Jesus while my godfather, John, prayed. It wasn't long before she left. My godfather said, "All is well." He said a covering prayer over me. I was still so afraid, so I slept up against my door. I didn't really sleep that night. I prayed and asked God for guidance. I couldn't go through something like this again. The next day I woke up early and I packed a bag. I had told the Bryant's that morning I was going to my friend's house for a party. They embraced and greeted me like last night never happened.

It was very weird for me as I was still feeling the after-effects of almost losing my life. So, Mrs. Bryant said, "Spring, I can bring you to work." I was very taken back by her offer, but then I remembered it was my payday and this was her norm. So, Mrs. Bryant is driving me to work and talking to Mr. Bryant all the way there. He says, "Don't forget to get our money out of her." Mrs. Bryant noticed I had not said anything the whole ride. She said, "We are still family despite our disagreements or fights. I still love you." I did not respond. So, Mrs. Bryant tells her husband, who is on the phone, "She is not responding. I can't stand her." She was starting to change, and I was getting scared again. Mr. Bryant said, "Bring her to the bank."

I finally opened my mouth and said, "Can I give it to you Sunday when I come back? I am going to be late for work." He said, "No. Now." So, we pulled up to the bank as usual, and I emptied my account. I was left with maybe 100 dollars. I was so angry, but I knew I was not returning to this house, so this would be the last thing they could every take from me. Mrs. Bryant dropped me off and said, "Have a lovely weekend. I'll pick you up on Sunday." I just closed the door.

When I entered work, I immediately emailed my boss and explained my situation. She told me about a crisis hotline that was available to me because I was an employee. She encouraged me to call them to see if there was anything they could do to help me. To my surprise, they were able to help me, but the only issue would be that I would have to go into a women's shelter in my area. I was so scared and terrified. I didn't want to go back to the Bryant's, so I went. With the scary new situation, I never went outside. I went to work and came back to the shelter. I was in this woman shelter for two full months. I saved and saved. When I left, I bought myself a gently used car and got my own place. I was able to furnish it with everything I needed like a bed, couch, TV, and other essential things. I finally felt like the storm in my life had passed and there were nothing but clear blue skies from here on out. But boy was I mistaken,

As I was resting in this new sense of peace that I had finally found, I met someone. He wasn't just any guy, Ahmad, was the first guy to ever see me. Yes! Just simply Spring. He called me by my name. I felt like he saw Spring for who I really was, not for what he could take from me. I fell for him instantly. Ahmad was the first guy to take me out or tell me I was beautiful. He showed me love and affection that I had never experienced before. Being with him was like being on cloud nine 24/7. I finally felt like I meant something to someone in this life. I finally had my ultimate protector. I thought I was his Bonnie and he was my Clyde; Jay to his Queen B. But that was far from the truth, I would discover. I ended up getting a new job offer in a different town with higher pay and better benefits. So, I ended up moving into a condo in the town where my new job was.

Ahmad told me he really didn't have a place to stay because he and his family members kept having altercations. I told AD (Ahmad) he could move in with me. For the first time, I felt like I was living. This was my first time living with a man on my own. My upbringing told me what I was doing was wrong, but I thought he was my husband and my soulmate. I did not believe he was an ungodly soul-tie. So, it's a few months into us being in our new home. Things were going great until AD got too comfortable with me. He asked me to go out with him to the club with his friends. I said, "I'm not into that. I'm a homebody." He said, "Can you get sexy for me and be my date?" For the first time, I had a man that admired me for my beauty, so I thought. Hey, why not? I went out and bought a nice outfit. It was nothing I would have ever worn, but he boosted my confidence. That night we came home from the club, and he was DRUNK.

I said, "AD. I really had a good time tonight." He said, "Why were you dancing with that other guy?" At first, I said, "What guy?" He said, "AT THE CLUB, SPRING!" I said, "It was fun and games. I'm with you." AD grab me by my neck and held me by pinning me to the wall. He whispered in my ear angrily, "DON'T EVER disrespect me ever again!" I am steady trying to explain while I have tears rolling down my eyes. He finally let me go, and I just dropped to the floor. I wasn't expecting this from him. I'm rethinking the whole night. I thought about how I was disrespecting him. I sat in the same spot for what seemed like hours. As the days went on, he tried to do everything to show me he was sorry. I just wasn't ok with him putting his hands on me. I accepted his apology because I truly loved AD.

The next situation that we went through I felt like life didn't prepare me for it. I went and had my yearly checkup. I had been feeling weak and tired more than usual. I started having tremors. My doctor said, "Ms. Taft, you're 2 ½ months pregnant." Immediately I wanted to know if the child was ok because I wasn't feeling my best. I was under a lot of stress. She said, "The baby is fine, Ms. Taft. But we will have to pull you off your seizure medication. We must find something that's safe for you and the baby. I really would like to place you on bed rest because this is a very high-risk pregnancy." I said, "Well, I can't leave my job."

I went home that evening so down because I didn't know how AD would take the information. When I came in, he had cooked dinner. He turned and looked at me; then I just broke down. He said, "What's wrong Spring?" I said, "I'm pregnant." He said, "Well, I wasn't trying to have any kids, but we must deal with the situation." Weeks passed by, and I had seizures after seizures out of my sleep; falling. My body was not taking this pregnancy thing ok. I passed out and had a grand mal seizure that night. I was admitted to the hospital. The doctors came in and said, "Ms. Taft, your body is rejecting the pregnancy. You're having a miscarriage." So, they did a procedure, but AD didn't stay in the hospital with me. He wanted to go back home. He had other things to tend to. A few days later, I was released from the hospital. I came home ANGRY. I was mad at God, myself, and AD.

Over the next couple of months, I just poured myself into my career at work. AD called me while I was at work and said, "Let's go out tonight. I'll pick you up something to wear. I'll come to get you." I said no at first but the last couple of months were rough for me, so I could use a night out and a drink. I just wanted to stay numb. I'm just being honest. So, when AD and his friends came to pick me up, it was evident that they had already started drinking. AD explained to me he lost his driver's license. We got to the club, and the bouncer said he couldn't come in. So, we ended up leaving. He said, "I just want to go to the strip club." I said, "I don't want to go." So, his friend Tiffany said, "Let's just chill at my house while the boys go out and have fun." I said, "Sure because I don't like going to the club anyway."

So, while I'm at Tiffany's house, she began to tell me how she and AD became friends. I was like, "Wow, that's a blessing!" I never knew we had that in common. The following day while AD was bringing me to work, I said, "AD. We need to share more. Tiff told me that me and you both experienced bullying. It's crazy how you can walk the same path as someone but in the situation feel like you're alone. You have me now." I grabbed his hand. AD immediately got angry and slapped me in my face while he was driving. That night when I got off work, he called his friend Tiff and said, "Did you tell her anything?" She said, "No." I said, "Why would she say that?" AD began to beat on me like never before while his friends were on speaker. I was being dragged from room to room screaming. At this point, I just gave up. I felt like I couldn't stop him. It felt like it went on for hours. He finally stopped. I just laid on the floor and cried out to God. First, my child. Now, me. I felt like I was being picked on.

The next day, I ended up mustering what little strength I had and made my way to church. The Apostle of the House was speaking in the prophetic. While I was worshiping, he said, "That man is not your husband." He just kept repeating it. I felt like I was being beaten in the spirit because I asked God for freedom from the Bryant's to go right back into bondage again. I left church, and I knew what I had to do. I went home that evening, and I told AD we couldn't live together anymore. AD did not take the news too great! We started to fight, he choked me out and said, "If he couldn't be with me then no one would." When he let me go, I tried to call the police. He smashed my phone. I said, "I just want you to go. I can't do this." As he walked out the door, he said, "Remember, what I told you."

The next day, I went out to run errands like I usually did. I was going down a hill, and I noticed that my car wouldn't stop. I kept slamming down on the brakes. The vehicle just accelerated. Now there was a car in front and behind me. I didn't want to hit the car in front of me because my car would have flipped. Also, if the car behind me would have hit me, I would have flipped. So, I merged right. What I could remember is when I woke up, I had already crashed head-on into a tree. When I got myself out of the car, all my airbags deployed. I got burned from my airbags, and my leg was hurt, but I didn't care. I immediately called AD. I said, "I just got into an accident.

Something happened with the brakes." He said, "What did I tell you?" then hung up. I called my mother Samantha and told her I got into an accident. By this time, the ambulance and paramedics were asking me if I was ok I said, "Yes." I explained the full situation the police officer.

She said, "You can't return to your home. I am making a referral for you to go to a domestic violence shelter, but it won't be around here." I said, "Ok." I went to the hospital. I was fine overall. Thank God He spared my life. My mother Samantha came and got me from the trauma center in the hospital. I told my mom her what happened and how he snapped. I asked, "Can I just come to your house. I don't want to go back to a women's shelter." She said, "No," because my older sister Riley was there with her son Peter." I felt devastated more so than I have ever been. "I can't go to my home!" I yelled angrily. So that following week, my mother Sam brought me back home. I packed my things, and I went to a domestic violence shelter three hours from where I lived.

Peace I leave with you, my peace I give unto you: not as the world giveth, give I unto you. Let not your heart be troubled, neither let it be afraid.— John 14:27

CHAPTER FOUR

Disconnect

To be disconnected there must be a break in the connection of some sort. In this season in my life, I felt like everything was disconnected from me such as my family, relationship, friends, and faith. It was like I was left on a small island all by myself. No one could reach me, but everyone could see me and knew I was on this island alone. I was now in the domestic violence (DV) shelter, and my state of mind was that of complete devastation. I could barely leave my room or even get out of my bed. At this point, I JUST wanted TO HIDE OUT TILL THIS STORM passed. But, unfortunately, I could not do that.

In the DV shelter, I was around all kinds of people. Women were there from all different walks of life. I was the youngest person. Many days, I would try to do something I would normally do like write and communicate with others. But at this point, my voice and my thoughts were disconnected. I couldn't say or do anything. I tried to regain my life. I tried to pick up the pieces from where I left off in my life. I tried to get back to myself, Spring! But this road to reconnection was anything from easy. I felt like my life was a utility bill that hadn't been paid, and until I pay the total amount owed, my service will be shut off. I was praying, but I couldn't feel God anymore. I would be up crying for many days. It was like I couldn't feel God or trace Him. It was as if our connection had been broken indefinitely. I didn't know how to reconnect. So, I just went on trying to live. I was trying to make it day by day.

I was trying to survive. I didn't know what the Bible was until I made it to this point in my life.

So, here I was in a new location. I had no job, car, or money. I tried to reach out to family members, but to no avail, no one ever answered. I felt like I was stuck and severely isolated. I felt like everyone was having the time of their life. I was just stuck there starving mentally, physically, and spiritually. I was bleeding out, and no one could help me. While being in this place, I met several women that took me in as their little sister. We talked about life's lessons, and we looked after each other. They imparted into me about the things they knew that, unfortunately, I did not. Because of my age, I had no experience or knowledge of it. They shared with me things that they have been going through and went through. It didn't make my situation seem so big where I felt like I was lost everything. I became grateful for the things I did have, like my life and stable health.

As I thought about how depressed and lost I was feeling, I could not imagine experiencing any of that with children. But many women in the DV shelter, that was their very situation. Some had more than one child. For some, English wasn't their first language, but I still tried my best to communicate with them. Being in this disconnected situation wasn't easy. I formed a mutual bond with the women in the DV shelter. We supported and prayed for each other. Most of all, we encouraged ourselves daily to continue living. Our stories didn't end here. We created new chapters in our lives. Having this connection with these women really brought joy and happiness back into my life. It was almost my time to leave the DV Shelter. I had saved up the little money I had from working my part-time job that I found in a town where I lived. But, of course, the enemy is always trying to trip me up.

I had got sick one night, and I had told one of the staff members at the time I didn't feel so well. As I'm telling the staff member this, it was like I couldn't see. My vision went completely black. I could no longer see the women anymore. The staff member walked out and said that it was not her problem. I began to cry out to God and said, "Why? Why? Why? You know I can't watch over myself if I pass out. I don't know what's going to happen, but she walked out so now I'm here alone." The women in the domestic violence shelter said about 20 minutes after she had left, I passed out. I had a grand mal seizure.

I was on the seventh floor of a 10-story building. At the time, the elevators were broken. The woman in the shelter began to call 911. The women didn't know the actual address to where the shelter was located. So, again, there were no staff members on duty. The dispatcher begins working with the women of the shelter. The dispatcher asked the woman several questions to try to do a bit of research to find out where the shelter was located. They finally figured out where we were in the safe house. Then they said, "Well, we have a problem. The elevator is down." "We can't get to her at this time," they said. I was still unconscious.

The EMT came up seven flights of stairs. By the time they had made it to me, I was coming out of the shock. I was a little disoriented and not really understanding what had just happened. But I could tell by the way my body felt that I had already knew. They asked me my name and a series

The Plug 65

of questions. For a while, I stayed silent because I was trying to process everything and get my bearing back together. I began to speak, but my speech was slurred. But over time, it got better after their evaluation. They said that I should go to the hospital. "We should take you just so that we can watch you overnight." I said, "No, I'm ok. I can stay." All the women in the shelter were concerned, and they were adamant that I should go.

So, I went. A few days later, I was released from the hospital. All my vital signs were fine. I was progressing well. I came back to the safe house. The same woman who walked out on me was the same woman that needed to apologize to me so she did not lose her job. She needed my forgiveness because now her job was on the line. I told her, "All is well." I said, "The enemy uses who he sees fit and yields themselves over to him."

It was move-in day for me, and I am overjoyed because I finally felt like God had smiled on me after being disconnected for four months from Him. Weeks prior, I found a church in the town where the safe house was. When I went, the man of God of the house immediately asked if he could speak what God was saying to me. I said, "God, Yes!" He said, "God, has you. This is all for your making. God is going to give you favor with a home in a residential area. You are going to go back to school for nursing. God has need of you in the kingdom of God." I just stood there and worshiped because for months, I thought I was being ignored, but God was listening. God was there with me the whole time.

So, it was move-in day. I got an apartment just 30 minutes outside of New York in a residential area. How it happened was a move of God because the landlord pursued me. I moved into the apartment immediately. So, I closed this chapter of my life. Learning and leaving with you, that even in your time of disconnection and period of silence from God, do not let go of His hands because your situation is for God's glory. So, endure the process.

Beloved, I wish above all things that thou mayest prosper and be in good health, Even as thy soul prospereth.— 3 John 1:2

CHAPTER FIVE

Static

STATIC means lacking in movement, action, or change, especially in a way viewed as undesirable or uninteresting. My life was all these things: lacking in movement, action, and change. I felt so undesirable and uninterested in life. I couldn't grasp living in my apartment. I thought this is what I wanted, and this is where I needed to be. I just needed to push forward and be in this place. If not, I would be back to where I was before the walls in my life collapsed before going into the shelter. There were times that I looked in the mirror and I didn't like the person that I saw. I couldn't even look at myself.

At this time, I was dealing with myself. It was the hardest thing because I was going to church, praying, and seeking God. I would spend countless days and hours thinking about who I was prior to my relationship. The more I thought about this pressing issue, I discovered that the old me was long gone. The innocent girl that only desired to help people and the pureness inside of me, I couldn't find it. I felt so ashamed and helpless. The press was really on. It felt like I had all this weight on me but not physical weight. It was spiritual weight like I was carrying around a full 5-pound backpack on my back. Now that's heavy! I went to sleep and woke up with the heaviness. I became accustomed to carrying my baggage. I continued to go to church, but honestly, I didn't feel a difference. I would praise God. But soon as I left the sanctuary, the heaviness would come back.

So, one night, I stayed up and wrote down everything that was on my mind. I nearly filled up my entire notebook. I laid on the floor that night crying in a ball for hours on hours. What I discovered was underneath all this heaviness that I was badly broken and bruised on the inside. This friction was keeping me from getting to the next level in God so much, so it was like I was spiritually hemorrhaging. I was dying from the inside out. The heaviness I was feeling was me trying to protect myself from the pain. I laid there helpless on my room floor examining myself. I felt the guilt, shame, and abandonment; the lack of value that I felt I had on the earth. I felt the disconnect from people, the lack of love, and the appreciation I wanted. I felt the abuse: verbally and physically.

I discovered that I still loved my ex even though he tried to end my life. I wanted him, but the root to that was being with my ex was my comfort. For the first time, I had found what I thought was love. I wanted love at all cost because without it at that time, I did not see value in myself. I needed my ex to complete me, so I thought. These things that I have been carrying, I didn't know how to let go of such as the issues with my mother, apparent daddy issues, and my self-esteem issues. I never knew how to release them. So, in the midst of my crying, I could hear God, but it wasn't clear. There was too much static in between His voice. It was like everything was far away, and our connection wasn't good.

At this point in my life, I was just at a standstill. I felt like I wasn't progressing. I was ultimately uninterested and disgusted with myself. Because I wasn't interested in anything, I was just trying to find myself in anything. I entered another relationship. Oh, yes. I know you're thinking, "How could you open one door, and you haven't closed the other?" Well, I was trying to mask the pain of my emotions. You should never mess with someone or do things out of emotion. You should never react out of emotion. You should give yourself time and let God heal you before you add in another person. I met this person, and finally, he's a man of God. He was everything that I thought I wanted. But, he was not anything that I needed at that time. So of course, Hamin and I hit it off immediately. Things went along great, and he took me out on a few dates. He cared about my hopes, dreams, and me staying in the will of God.

The Plug

One-night Hamin came over. I cooked and we watch a few movies. I fell asleep, and the enemy came in tempting my flesh. Hamin asks, "Can I stay over and take you out for breakfast in the a.m.?" I said, "Sure, but we are not going there. I am just not ready yet." He asks, "Can I just hold you till you fall asleep?" I said, "Yes." Unfortunately, I fell into temptation that night. We both acted out of emotion every time we saw each other. It got to a point where he blamed me. He said, "You're supposed to be a leader. How can you lead with unclean hands?" I would get so angry with him, and asked, "Why are you saying it like you were not here?" He said, "I know, but you're greater than this. Your anointing is too great for me ever to get comfortable with this." He repeated this almost daily to me. I felt like I'm not ready for whatever he is talking about. Why can't he drop it? I felt like it was my fault. I was doing something wrong, so I finally said to him, "You know, maybe I am the problem. Maybe I am the cause. Maybe you don't need to be with me right now."

So, Hamin and I ended up breaking up for a few months. Maybe six months later, we ended up re-connecting. He said, "Oh, you know I miss you. You know I still believe in you and us." Being with him was like we had twin spirits. He understood me in ways that no one has ever done before. We ended up dating once again, and we ended up coming close to falling from grace again. I said to him, "Wait, Hamin! We CAN'T!" I prayed to God that night and asked God to take the desires of lust away from me. I asked Him to touch me and deliver not just my soul but my heart. I asked Him if He could place me in a season where he could make me to be the woman of God, He desired me to be. I said, "I can't continue to mask my emotions on top of my pain with more pain and shame." Because eventually, I would have to deal with everything that I have locked up inside suppressed from the world but not from myself. It would be 10x times worse because I would have to get through what I went through and what I'm going through now.

Plus, I would have to also process yet another person out of my system. What people don't tell you is that every time you have sex with someone, you build a soul tie with that person. Your flesh will desire and yearn for something it does not need. But often than not, we succumb to these urges and desires. They place us, sometimes, in horrible or unhealthy situations spiritually. So, I prayed, and I began to get in my Word. I asked God to take away all the desires. For a long time, I didn't go on Facebook. I didn't take pictures. I didn't do anything. I just wanted to pray and get into God's presence because I didn't want to develop any generational curses that may have been on my family or maybe in my bloodline. I just wanted to be the woman of God that He called me to be.

So, I prayed this simple prayer: "Lord, thank You for blessing me. Lord, Father God, I ask that You forgive me for all my sins. Lord, Father God, I ask that You purify my heart. Oh God, I ask that You renew my mind. Oh God! Let this mind be in You, God, that is also with me in Christ Jesus! But I ask that You continue to walk with me hand in hand. Oh, God, I ask that You drive the desires away so that I am walking in Your will for my life. Search my heart and take out anything inside of me that is not healthy or conducive to my growth and development in You. God, I ask that You pull out my purpose that is locked up inside of me. God, I call forth the many gifts and callings You have placed on my life in the name of Jesus. God, I ask that You stir up the gift inside of me. Let it be like a fire which burns and consumes anything that is not like You. God, I ask that You invoke purpose and direction for my tomorrow. I am asking You to give me divine direction. God, I give You thanks for all the many blessings in my life. God, I submit myself over to You completely. God, I repent and ask You to forgive me for all my sins. God, I ask that You purify and sanctify me. Holy God, I ask that You renew my mind. Let this mind be in me that is also in Christ Jesus. God, I ask that You walk with me, hand in hand, so that I don't fall astray. God, I ask that You protect me from the enemy and myself. God, I ask that You change my desires and appetite. Let me begin to eat manna from heaven's table. God, whatever is a hindrance or a stumbling in my life that's blocking my destiny and purpose in You, I ask that you remove it in Jesus' mighty name. God, I ask that You mend the relationships in my family. Restore the joy. Take away the pain and guilt. God, I ask that You let me be an example to more people of what a godly lifestyle looks like. God, show me what my identity is in You. God, I ask that You give me a boldness to possess and walk in my inheritance that You have for me. All these things I ask in Your Son Jesus' name. Amen."

When you're in a season that you feel you are not moving, refer to God's Word. Standstill and submit yourself back to God. Find the source of the issues in your life that's causing static and friction between you hearing God's Word for your life.

But as for you, ye thought evil against me; but God meant it for my good, to bring to pass, as it is this day to save much people alive.— Genesis 50:20

CHAPTER SIX

New Sound

The word sound is defined as vibrations that travel through the air or another medium. Sound is produced by continuous and regular vibrations, as opposed to noise. Well, this chapter is called "New Sound" because everything in my life was hypertensive. There was a constant calm voice that I heard through all the vibrations. I moved from where I currently was living to be closer to my birth mother. I found a condo around the corner from where she lived. I thought by me being closer that it would allow our relationship to go further.

Right before I had moved, I was given a wonderful opportunity at a major financial company where I was living. They hired me to be the lead manager in their analytics department. I finally felt like I was in a place in my life or season of happiness and good luck. I felt untouchable because I was doing so well. I was hearing from God more and more. That New Year, I heard God say, "Get settled. Join the church that you had been visiting for a while." I didn't join that New Year's night. A few weeks later, I joined. I was so excited because everyone at the church was so inviting. I finally felt like I was at home in a church. I haven't felt this way since I was younger.

So that Monday, I went to work as I always do, cheerful and ready to see Friday! On Monday, the CEO wanted to meet with all the managers and supervisors, per usual. But unfortunately, this meeting was anything but normal. The CEO let us all know that the company would be merging with another existing financial company. Because of this, a lot of changes would be happening in the coming months with the company. Certain departments wouldn't exist anymore. He went on to say that the new company would also be bringing in some of their own people. So, I stood up and asked, "What would happen to my department?" He said, "Unfortunately, the company was coming in with highly advanced and experienced analyst. We would not need two departments doing the same thing." I asked, "So how long do we have exactly?" He stated, "Three months."

I walked out of the meeting devastated. I just was starting to feel like I was finally getting my life back together and, bam, another situation. But most importantly, I was so upset. I had to tell my teammates that after three months we would no longer have employment there. Mostly everyone on my team was well older than me. People had families and parents they cared for. My heart just broke. For a while, I did not tell anyone about my financial situation because I didn't want the judgment.

So, the three months came, and my company hosted a major farewell party, but I was not in a celebrating mood. I thought about how I was going to get through this situation. I still was going to church, and every time I went, God arrested me in the spirit. The Holy Ghost would hit me so bad. I would have no choice but to surrender how I felt to God. I would leave church with hope, instead of becoming dismayed after being catch up in the Holy Ghost.

While on my job hunt, I heard the Lord tell me clearly, "Start your Business/Ministry." I said, "God, but I'm broke. I am barely keeping gas in my car." He said, "Start it NOW!" While in the midst of putting my business together, I linked back up with an old friend that I knew before I went away to college. Her name was Jasmine, but everyone called her Jazzy. While catching up, Jazzy had told me how she needed my help with something. I said, "Sure. What would I be helping you with Jazzy?" She said, "I am getting a foster daughter, but she needs some guidance and mentorship." Jazzy said, "I would also pay you." I agreed because at the time I had no other income coming in.

So, the following week, I met my first mentee. Her name was Shoqunana, and just like her name sounds, she was extremely outgoing like she was getting ready for A SHOW. Jazzy said, "Spring, meet Shoqunana." I said, "A pleasure to meet you." Shoqunana and I sat down, and we began to talk. I realized that we had a lot in common; not just our rough upbringing, but also our passion and love for all music. Every day, Jazz would call me and say, "I am leaving to work can you come over to make sure Qunana gets off to school?" I would get to Jazz's house at 6:15 a.m.

Although technically I was working, it didn't feel like work. I got Qunana off on her school bus and wished her well. I was free until about 2 pm when Qunana would get home from school. Shoqunana was a 15-year-old multi-talented individual. When Qunana came home, I would have to bring her to work at the local McDonald's. Although she was young, she could only work 3-4 hours a day. So around 5 pm, I would pick Qunana up from work.

I built a big sister relationship with Qunana. She trusted me. I advised her about the many mistakes that I made in my life. I told her how because of my constant disobedience to God, I kept losing an already fixed game called LIFE. Qunana would tell me the things she had gone through in her life. Although I've never experienced those same things, I had compassion for her. Qunana told me her hopes and dreams for her future. There was just one thing that Qunana felt was holding her back. She was 15 and pregnant. Qunana didn't want her child to be born to the same system she fell victim to. My heart bled for her as a woman, child, and mom. I told her that she had all the capabilities to be a great mother but she would have to push herself.

That evening, I came back over to my friend Jazzy's house. When I arrived, Qunana and Jazz were in a heated argument. Jazz was saying some awful things that one should never say to anyone, let alone a child. I could feel the tension in the air of the house. I just began to pray.

"Lord, calm the storm. Lord, arrest them both. Let them begin to speak of love and not out of their emotions or anger. In Jesus' name, Amen." So Jazzy begins to threaten Qunana, and the argument takes a turn for the worse. To avoid and escalate the situation, Qunana ran out of the house, but she forgot her bag. When Qunana came back, she banged on the door. My friend Jazzy did something unexpected. She ran outside and tried to hit Qunana with a shovel. At this point, I was uncomfortable being there and the actions of my friend wasn't that of a mother or a mature adult. Seeing all of this, paralyzed me. It reminded me of things in my life that I had been through. Sometimes in life, God will shake things up and shift things so that you can begin to walk on the road called purpose, or on the highway called destiny.

Remember ye not the former things, neither consider the things of old. Behold I will do a new thing; now it shall spring forth; shall ye not know it? I will even make a way in the wilderness, and the rivers in the desert.— Isaiah 43:18-19

CHAPTER SEVEN

Melody

Melody is defined as a sequence of notes coming together to make a beautiful sound. Well at this point in my life, things were finally coming together and halfway making sense. There was a knock at the door. It was two police officers: one male and the other was a female. Behind them, I see Qunana. The officers asked, "Are you this child's legal guardian?" I said, "No. My friend Jazz is." The police officers asked if they could come in. I said, "Sure, why not?" They asked me did I know that I could be charged with a felony crime because the minor was kicked out of the house and threatened. I said, "Honestly, I'm just the child's mentor. My friend Jazz is her foster mother." The officers asked if I could step outside with them. I said, "Yes." He said, "Ma'am. Do you have an ID?" I politely answered, "Yes, I do. Just allow me one moment," as I went to grab it. As I came back on the porch, the officers began to ask me questions about what happened with the altercation between Jazz and Qunana. He said, "I do want to let you know that if you withhold information, that is involving a minor, you will be charged and that would be a felony."

So, I began to tell him what I observed happened as I was pulling up to the house and what happened with both parties involved. The police officer then asked me. "Can you tell me what happened outside?" I told the police officer the truth which was that Jazz got out of character and came outside. She tried to hit Qunana in the head with the shovel. The officer said, "That's all I needed to know." While all this was going on, I was texting and trying to call Jazz. At this point, she was avoiding my phone calls and my text messages. Later that night, I got a text from

Jazz that her boyfriend had taken her out to the casino. She said that she was close to the shore and she didn't have great reception. She said that she wouldn't be home until Monday and that I needed to get Qunana off to school. She asked if I wouldn't mind staying with her for the whole weekend. Because I was already at Jazz's house, I said yes. But I didn't know at the time, what I was really saying yes to. Monday came in like any other school day for a child. I woke Qunana up. I helped her get ready and off to school, so I thought.

Around 11 a.m., I received a phone call from Jazz. She was hysterical. "Did you make sure she got on the bus and went to school?" I said, "Of course I did. I walked outside with her, and I made sure she boarded the bus." "My friend just stated, Spring, that she jumped off the bus. She still in town somewhere." So, because Qunana and I had a rather very good big sister relationship, I knew all her little spots. So, I began to call her phone. She did not answer. I started to pull up at her spots. At the first one, she wasn't there, but at the second location, she was there.

I told Qunana's boyfriend to go inside and retrieve her for me because I needed to speak with her right away. He stated to me, "Oh, she's not here with me." I said, "I just pinged her phone to your location. If you would like, I can contact the police and the authorities. They can come to pick her up. I just need to talk to her and ask her why she felt the need to skip school." Ten minutes later Qunana walked outside. She was really upset and didn't want to talk to me. After she calmed down, she explained that she didn't want to go to school and that she didn't want to live with my friend Jazz anymore. She stated how she was stressed out being pregnant and living in an already stressful situation by being a foster child. She just didn't want to go back. I said, "Qunana, well, what are your options? I don't know your situation."

Long story short, I entered a new chapter in my life. I contacted Qunana's social workers and her team that works closely with her. They agreed to let me become Qunana's new foster mother. This was something I had never done before. It was something I could only dream about, which was having my own daughter. I instilled in her the things that I've learned thus far in my life, but it was more than that, it was a journey. It was my assignment God had placed me on. So, a sequence of different events was coming together for me and putting me on the road to my purpose and on my way to my destiny.

By now, I am a certified business owner, of YouthfullyInspired4Real Youth Ministries, LLC. I was so proud of myself, genuinely for the first time. I was completely satisfied with doing what I was doing. On Sunday, my daughter and I headed to the temple. Praise and worship had already begun. I walked in and, again, God arrested me in the Spirit. I began to praise God so hard that my daughter began to embrace me. I told her that I was ok, and I just love worshiping God.

The next thing I knew, Qunana took off praising God. Of course, I could not let my baby girl praise God by herself, so I joined in. We went all out for God that Sunday. We did not even know it was youth Sunday and that Youth Pastor Chris was preaching. What a mighty word it was. He spoke on being part of the chosen generation. He said that you can be chosen and have made several mistakes, but that does not take away God's word He spoke over your life. When he was done with his message, this woman walks up to sit next to my daughter and me. This young Prophetess began to speak into my life as the service was going on. She starts telling me things that no one knew about me. I began to weep because I knew this was God speaking through her. She then begins to tell me the many places God was going to take me and that He was going to use me in a mighty way. She then embraced me with a huge and left. I sat there for a while and just worshiped God for the word of confirmation that I had just received. As I lifted my head up, I saw that Youth Pastor Chris had called an altar call for the young people.

Guess who is up at the altar? YUP! My baby girl walked herself up to get prayer. I left from my seat, went and stood in agreement with what the man of God was praying over her. On this day Shoqunana, received God for herself from what she witnessed me do in front of her. My lifestyle, though I wasn't rich, all my needs were met currently. I took care of Qunana for a long time before she got placed into a permanent situation.

But the life lessons I instilled in her will be with her for a lifetime. I was also able to take away from her being my daughter is that there is a melody and a note in every string of life. You must listen for it. At this point, everything in my life was coming together like a sweet melody; one I couldn't stop listening to.

The Lord thy God in the midst of thee is mighty; he will save, he will rejoice over thee with joy; he will rest in his love, he will joy over thee with singing.— Zephaniah 3:17

CHAPTER EIGHT

Connection

The definition of connection is a relationship in which a person, thing or idea is LINKED in some way. Let me say the connection was rapid and unexpected, but extremely worth it. It's the day before I said my final goodbyes to my foster daughter, Qunana. It was hard for both of us. The young single mother's program she was entering would help her go to college and gain the skills she needed to be an independent parent. I watched Qunana leave, but I was excited about her new journey and mines as well. Suddenly, everything in my life started to come together like a major puzzle. But the story didn't end there. As I stood before God, He advised me to start my own business/ministry. At this time, I was just working on the knowledge that I had learned in college which was marketing and self-branding. Honestly, I always saw myself as a background person, not front and center. But at this point, I felt like God was pulling me to the forefront.

I started my first project, "Youth Encounter 2K19." While planning for my first youth encounter, God sent another messenger to deliver me my next assignment. This assignment pushed me in the direction of my destiny. Although it was scary, it was something that I've never done before, but ultimately, I had to take the leap of faith. A few weeks after Qunana had left, I went to take care of my grandmother while my mother and aunt went out of town for two weeks. I stayed with my grandmother at her house. While I was taken care of her, my grandmother and I shared in many moments where we worshiped and watched The Word Network on my laptop. While all this was going on, I heard the Lord tell me, "Prepare for relocation." I said Lord, "I can't leave my GG." He said, "I have her, but it's your time and season." I kept praying to God because I knew what He was requesting of me. I just did not know at the time if I could complete the task.

It's now two weeks later and my mom and aunt were back from their trip. I returned to my apartment only to find out that my apartment had flooded. Everything I owned, at this point, was ruined. Over the next couple of days, I cleaned and threw stuff out of my apartment. But unfortunately, it was inhabitable. Now usually I would get upset and be saddened because something like this happened. But it was all according to God's grand plan for my life. So, because I trusted Him, I put my trust and faith in Him alone. I did not let this situation make my faith wavier.

So, I reconnected with my spiritual mother, Mia, who I had met long ago. She had been teaching, "How to Seek God Even in a Hard Place." She taught me how to fast and pray. Mia and I fasted for a week. It was the first time regarding my next assignment. I got a call at almost midnight. My spiritual mother, Mia, said, "Would you like to come out to the mid-west and help with the ministry?" Immediately, I heard God said, "Go." Twenty minutes later my ticket was purchased, and I was on my way to Minnesota.

Docking in Minnesota was peaceful, but I kept hearing God say, "You're on an assignment. Stay focused, Spring. Do not get off track." Mia explained to me that she would be going overseas for a while for ministry purposes and she needed me to stay at her Condo with her oldest daughter Brayalynn. I was super excited for the first couple of days while God had me adjusting to being in the mid-west. I fasted just so I could hear from God. That Sunday, Mia brought me to her church. This Bishop of the house asked me to minster that Sunday. There was only one problem; my voice was so sore. Mia stepped up for me and told him yes before I could say anything.

As I walked up to greet the Church, I was nervous, but there was a unique sound that I released out my mouth. People began to worship and praise God. I even got caught up and lost in worship. It was an intoxicating experience, in a good way. It felt as though God had poured

Himself out on me and spoke through me. Well, it was finally the next week, and Mia is leaving to travel overseas. I brought her to the airport. She prayed with me and said, "I'm only one call away. It's time you get ready to walk into your destiny."

Mia was now gone for a few weeks, and her daughter, Lynn, and I were bonding. Lynn would even help me work out when she wasn't at work. We would talk about life, the future, and her faith in God. It was a couple of days before my birthday, and I heard the Lord tell me to go on a three day dry fast. Instead of giving God three days only, I extended and sacrificed my birthday by laying before Him. So I fasted for a total of five full days. Five means God's grace that He has towards me. The Lord said, "Spring, let this be a dry fast. Nothing. No water. No food. Let me feed you, mouth to mouth." Now at this point, I never did a dry fast. It seemed hard when I thought about it, but I had faith that I could complete it.

So, its day one. I locked myself in my room. I anointed myself, laid before God, and allowed Him to pour into me. It was a refreshing feeling. God would wake me up a couple of hours (12 a.m

., 3 a.m., 6 a.m., 12 p.m.) to pray and worship before Him. Even at times when I felt weak, and I could not press forward, God allowed me to rest in His presence. I would have visions, and God would speak to me through my dreams. The second to last day before my fast was over, God woke me up that morning. I prayed and worshiped God like I normally did. But only this time God's sweet presence showed up in a mighty way. I started to speak in new tongues. My tears began to flow as I worshiped and praised God like never before. God began to download into me who I was and why He called me. God explained to me exactly what He needed me to do. I remembered God speaking to me like this years ago when I was on the bus, but only this time, it was much clearer. I got a full understanding of my purpose.

The last day of my fast was my birthday. My god sister Lynn wanted to know if I could bring her to Walmart to shop. I said, "Sure," thinking I would be off my fast in a few hours. While in the store, Lynn and myself grabbed things that we needed for the house. We also talked. She stated how she prayed for me while I was fasting. She knew it was hard but would be worth it in the end for me.

Lynn and I arrived at the checkout counter. I put my phone down for two seconds to help unload the cart. We were checking out, and Lynn asked me, "Where is your phone?" I turned around and said, "Right here," but my phone was gone! I began to panic! I said, "Lynn, my phone was right here." Lynn said, "Let me try to locate your phone with the Find my iPhone App." I said, "Yes!" So, I logged all my information into Lynn's phone to locate my phone but unfortunately, the app was saying my phone was disabled. I started to pray out loud in the store. "The devil is a liar! I bind every witch, warlock, and every unclean spirit working against me at this very moment." Then the Lord said, "Spring, go look back where you first laid your phone."

So, I walked back over in the line, and I found my phone turned off in the candy box. Lynn and I proceed to walk out of Walmart, thanking and praising God. The next morning, my fast was over. I prayed and anointed myself. The refill that God gave my heart and soul would be an experience that I will never forget. I gave birth to my purpose in those five days. My spiritual mother, Mia's mom cooked for me in celebration of my birthday. We had a little get together at her house. I was so excited not just because I could finally eat, but because I finally found my purpose in God. This was the celebration of my new-found identity in Christ.

It was finally the week Mia was coming home. Just before she docked back into the US, my sister Lynn lost her best friend. When she got the call, I just stood there and began to pray for her. Lynn was very broken up behind this tragic event. Because God saw me through a season like this more than once, I just encouraged her. I said, "It is ok to be sad, but do not stay in this place because we know that nothing happens on this earth without God's knowledge or authority. Nothing happens that is not according to God's will or grand plan. We must continue to trust God. Know it's all working out for our good."

Mia was back in town with only days before her brother's wedding. I was so excited, but God had been speaking to me on my next assignment.

He said that I would be relocating back to the east coast. God had spoken this word over me earlier this year, but I was unsure as to how it was all going to play out. God said to me that I would be attending and helping in the ministry at Abundant Life International Ministry (ALIM) were the Pastor is Clayton Reynolds, a world-renowned pastor, and speaker. I said, "God, I don't have the finances to step out. God said, "Trust me. The way has already been made."

It was the day of the wedding, and I was celebrating with the bride and groom on their new union, but I was also celebrating about the fact of this assignment in my life was over. I could look forward to a new journey and greater doors opening with God. I truly enjoyed myself at the wedding. I did not know that in just three days, I would be leaving my spiritual mom, Mia, my god siblings, and the church I was working in. God made a way; my ticket was purchased. I headed to leave out that evening, but before I could travel to my destination, I asked God, "Is this what You desire for me to do?" God simply answered me with, Luke 10:1, "After these things the Lord appointed other seventy also; and sent them two and two before his face into every city and place, whither he himself would come."

I said, "yes, Lord, I will obey," before I knew it, I was in my new location. I arrived at my new location on a Sunday. The only thing God did not reveal to me was where I would be staying. Let's just say God worked it all out in days. Matter of a fact, it was hours. I arrived at the first apartment complex that I was planning to live. Immediately things worked out. My application was accepted. Guess what? I was not required to place a down payment on my new home. This apartment condo was better than the one that I previously lived in. I had a two-bedroom, two-bathroom condo with a deck, and a fireplace. I felt like I had stepped into my wealthy place. The manager at the apartment complex said that I could move in just a few days. In the meantime, God established me shelter in a nearby hotel until my home was ready.

It was finally the day of my interview with ALIM. I woke up early that morning, prayed, and laid before the Father. As I pulled up to the church, a sense of relief had come over me. I knew I was walking in with my two greatest weapons:

Jesus and the Holy Ghost. After only being in the meeting for less than 15 minutes they could tell I was perfect for the position. I was hired on the SPOT! I was so excited, and I wanted to break into a praise in the office, but I held on to it. The Director of the department that I was going to be working in let me know what the onboarding procedure would be. She also asked if I would be available in the next few days for training. I immediately told her YES! It was finally move-in day, and I was so excited because I finally had my own space and my own place. It was better than the one I lost. I was so grateful.

In the coming weeks, I worked at the church in my new position. I was so excited because I loved my interaction with all the kids that I took care of. I should have expected that the enemy would try me in this season. I was just so caught up in the joy of the moment that I was unaware of the attack that was coming.

While transitioning to my new location, I lost some of my important documents. I advised my Director of this situation, and I let her know I could provide her with the copies until my originals came in which I had just ordered. She advised me that I could not give her copies and let her know when my originals come in. I continued to work until a week before my paperwork came in. My director told me that I could not return to work until I had all my proper paperwork. I pleaded with her to see if they would accept my copies until the originals came in. She stated, "No." Unfortunately, My Director also advised me that I had one week from that date to provide them with my paperwork or I would be terminated. I hung up my phone feeling so defeated.

I went before God and asked Him to expedite my paperwork. I did not want to lose my position. That Tuesday, I received another call from my Director. She asked, "Spring, do you have all your necessary paperwork we requested?" I said, "No. You said that you were given me a week, this coming Thursday, and it's only Tuesday?" She said, "Unfortunately, Spring, we are going to have to terminate you because we do not have your paperwork." I kept repeating, "You said a week." Then I asked, "Well when my papers get here, can I get my position back?" She stated that it was not up to her, but I had to contact HR. The conversation ended. I felt as if my heart had dropped to my feet. The next day, all my documents came in the mail. I was so excited that I immediately reached out to my Director to let her know. I was unable to reach her, so that Sunday, before I attended service, I stopped by my job. I spoke with one of the other directors who said that my Director would be in touch with me. I left church feeling hopeful. I did not know that I was entering another familiar testing season.

That Monday, I received a call from my sister at 7 a.m. I saw that she had called me several times. I felt the urgency to call her back as I said, "Hello," I knew something was wrong. My older sister began to scream in my ear, "She's GONE! She's GONE!"

I am trying to understand exactly what's happening. She tells me that my grandmother who was my number one supporter had transitioned from this world to the kingdom of God. I just held the phone, and a wave of emotions hit me all at once. I told my sister, "It was her time. GG is at peace now. We must carry on her legacy."

In the next coming weeks, I returned home to be with my mother and siblings as we laid my grandmother to rest. On the day of my grandmother's service, I was filled with so many emotions. I was relieved that my GG left her earthly vessel for wings and pearls forever. My GG's service and sendoff were amazing. We celebrated her just as she celebrated so many others. During the closing remarks, I heard the Lord say, "Speak to My people and provide them with hope."

As I approached the pulpit, I asked the Lord to speak through me and give me the exact words to say. I encouraged my family to build a personal relationship with God. I encouraged them not to let their alarm ring and they no longer have the time to prepare or fix things now. I said, "Whatever you are facing, God can heal and deliver you from it. You must believe and submit yourself back to God." In the coming days, I knew I had to prepare myself to return home. I had a conversation with God and asked, "What am I returning home to? I have no furniture in my home. I have no income." God simply said, "Trust Me." I said, "Yes, Lord."

As I traveled back home, God began to take me back through the last ten years of my life. God said, "I've created things to work out for your good and for Me to get the glory in the end. I've designed and hand-picked every testing season to shape and mold you into the person you were created to be. I need you to have a Face-to-Face encounters with Me. I needed to cut out all the distractions in your life. I needed to know if you really trusted Me like you said you did. So many people say they trust Me, but when put to the test, it's proven that they trust Me with earthly limitations." As, God is speaking to my spirit, I began to cry out and slip into deep worship because, in my desert and dry place, He was my LIVING WELL.

So, as I close this chapter in my life, I leave you with this, "P.L.U.G. in!" Let nothing or no one keep you from connecting and experiencing God in all His glory. God took a broken, beaten, battered, whoremonger, with abandonment issues and low self-esteem. God said, "Spring is fit for the kingdom of God. I can use her. I shall call her Prophetess. She shall be a glory carrier for

My name's sake." How much more can God do and perform in your life? It does not matter what path or road you find yourself walking down. Now is the TIME TO SURRENDER and PLUG IN. God needs you. God still sees you as valuable to Him. It's time for you to step into your kingdom inheritance. Someone is waiting to be saved and waiting to be helped, but it is all predicated on your obedience. Are you willing to submit yourself over to God? Will you connect to P.L.U.G.?

Surely he shall not be moved forever: the righteous shall be in everlasting remembrance. He shall not be afraid of evil tidings: his heart is fixed, trusting in the Lord. His heart is established, he shall not be afraid, until he sees his desire upon his enemies.— Psalms 112:6-8

Conclusion

In life, we are all are searching for a sense of belonging, a place to call home, or a place where unconditional love can flow. Peace and understanding can help aid us into the person that we are destined to be. Ultimately, a place of healing where we can grow and develop into the person that God has purposed us to be. God gave me this phrase, and it merely says, "Dream + Vision + Purpose = Lifestyle." It's simple and means God gives or allow us to have dreams which will lead to a vision and a God-given road map to our purpose, which should be something we should be aiming for in our daily lives. So many times, we get stuck in repeated seasons and cycles that we fail to make the connection with God. 3 John 1:2 says, "Beloved, I wish above all things that thou mayest prosper and be in health, even as thy soul prospereth."

God does not desire for us as His children to become estranged and disconnected from Him. Imagine being a parent and giving birth to a child who you carried for over nine months. As the child grows and develops, he or she desires not to connect or can't find a way to communicate with you as their parent. So, as a parent, you begin to feel rejected, unwanted, or unappreciated. It's the same way with God. He does not like when we as His children reject Him. Rather not talk with Him when just like a parent, He is waiting there to fix and heal all our many situations.

Psalms 145:18-19 says, "The Lord is near to all who call on him, to all who call on him in truth. He fulfills the desires of those who fear him; he hears their cry and saves them."

All we must do is call upon the Lord. He will answer with love and strength, not with judgment. It was in those moments when I surrendered and cried out to God that I was completely at peace. I took solace in the fact that through all my many ups and downs, God has stayed consistent, and been my anchor through it all. Habakkuk 1:5 (NIV) says, "Look at the nations and watch and be utterly amazed. For I am going to do something in your days that you would not believe, even if you were told." Even if God were to tell me how great and marvelous my life would be even after each season, or if He allowed someone to speak it into my life, I would have laughed and rejected the word. Like the prophet Habakkuk, I would have looked at my current situation through my natural eyes instead of with my spiritual eyes. At that point, I had not figured out how to PLUG-IN. Connecting to God and fixing your connection to Him is so important.

2 Corinthians 12:9 says, "But he said to me, "My grace is sufficient for you, for my power is made perfect in weakness." Therefore, I will boast all the more gladly about my weaknesses, so

that Christ's power may rest on me." What God is simply saying in this Scripture is that He is not looking for perfect people. He is NOT looking for someone who has it together every day or all day. But He is looking for people who can make a conscious decision and commit to working on a better connection with Him daily. What I have learned from the many seasons that I've been through is that God created in me everything I need to plug-in and connect to God authentically. If I was to connect to God illegally, I would be an electric fire waiting to happen.

When He created me, He wrote in His Word in Philippians 1:6, "Being confident of this very thing, that He who hath begun a good work in you will perform it until the Day of Jesus Christ." God is saying to us that He has given us a promise that we can hold on to. You may not be in the place where you think you should be, but if you hold on and put your trust in Him, you will see that everything is working towards your good. God is putting you under the refiner's fire in the pain and the suffering. There is a purification that happens in these moments. Let's think about it. Imagine trying to charge your phone with a broken charger. No matter how much you tape this wire, the connection is broken. So, instead of going to buy another wire and renewing your connection, you continue to repeat the same method, that has not led you to a connection or charge. You have not come to grips that the power cord has become deactivated permanently. It has become defective and dead!

A lot of times, we, as believers, try to connect with God based on how we connect with our spouses, children, friends, etc. We judge God based upon those relationships. So, when God does not respond like we think He should, we become petty with Him! Myself included. We get into our emotions and start trying to walk out our own soul or salvation without the common denominator, which is JESUS. Then we end up in situations and misfortunes that causes us to come running back to God. Like the great parent He is, He never judges us. He picks us up and establishes us on our feet in the position towards our purpose in Him.

Like the woman who had the issue of blood for 12 years, she was picked on and labeled dirty and filthy. She was viewed as an unclean woman. If you read the story in depth, you will discover the woman used up all her financial resources to cure her issue. To no avail, she was unable to get her situation fixed. This woman had no friends, so she was isolated and abandoned. She lacked financially and on top of that, she was suffering in her body. Honestly, this was God's second demonstration of a "JOB" situation. But the woman with the issue of blood did not let her situation disrupt her connection with God. She fought through a crowd of people to touch the HEM of JESUS' garment. According to the Scripture, there was a mob of people around JESUS. Anyone of them could have touched Him, but there was something about this woman's connection. The BIBLE records that JESUS felt virtue leave His body. The definition of virtue is behavior showing high moral standards. It goes on to say righteousness, uprightness, integrity, honesty, and worthiness. So, out of all the people around JESUS at this time, no one possessed this one characteristic. The one they called dirty, and the one they looked over, was the one who was desperate enough to connect with God despite her situation.. The woman with the issue of blood did not let what people said, or her outward appearance stop her from reaching JESUS. She needed to GET connected to her healer, her source, and her EVERYTHING.

God left the masses to save and heal the ONE, you. What we should take from this passage in the Bible is that no matter what our circumstances are, or no matter what we are facing currently, we should be hungry for a pure connection to God. We should seek to have a relationship with God more than we seek gossip, lying, backbiting, jealousy, envy, sexual desires, etc. Because one touch from God can change the whole trajectory of your life, for instance, look at me. I am an example. That one moment in the Master's hands can change you forever. Let's go one step further. Sometimes, we feel we can not perfect our connection with God because people have seen us in our valley season. So, if we do anything contrary to what they have witnessed, judgment falls, and condemnation sets in. I want us to look at three instances where labels held these people back, but God still chose to connect with these people. Let start with Mark 5:1-20 (NIV).

"They went across the lake to the region of the Gerasenes. When Jesus got out of the boat, a man with an impure spirit came from the tombs to meet him. This man lived in the tombs, and no one could bind him anymore, not even with a chain. For he had often been chained hand and foot, but he tore the chains apart and broke the irons on his feet. No one was strong enough to subdue him. Night and day among the tombs and in the hills he would cry out and cut himself with stones. When he saw Jesus from a distance, he ran and fell on his knees in front of him. He shouted at the top of his voice, "What do you want with me, Jesus, Son of the Most High God? In God's name don't torture me!" For Jesus had said to him, "Come out of this man, you impure spirit!" Then Jesus asked him, "What is your name?" "My name is Legion," he replied, "for we are many." And he begged Jesus again and again not to send them out of the area. A large herd of pigs was feeding on the nearby hillside. The demons begged Jesus, "Send us among the pigs; allow us to go into them." He gave them permission, and the impure spirits came out and went into the pigs. The herd, about two thousand in number, rushed down the steep bank into the lake and were drowned. Those tending the pigs ran off and reported this in the town and countryside, and the people went out to see what had happened. When they came to Jesus, they saw the man who had been possessed by the legion of demons, sitting there, dressed and in his right mind; and they were afraid. Those who had seen it told the people what had happened to the demon-possessed man and told about the pigs as well. Then the people began to plead with Jesus to leave their region. As Jesus was getting into the boat, the man who had been demon-possessed begged to go with him. Jesus did not let him, but said, "Go home to your own people and tell them how much the Lord has done for you, and how he has had mercy on you." So, the man went away and began to tell in the Decapolis how much Jesus had done for him. And all the people were amazed.

No one wanted to be connected to this man. They did not even want to see about him. But God saw the man was tormented and freed him. Jesus did not look upon him with disgust or shame. This is a powerful tool of how the love of God has so much compassion for us, even in our darkest hour. Jesus told the man, "Run! Go and tell all the people who has just saved you." What God is looking for is to get the glory out of your situation no matter how bad it may look. You may have had an abortion, committed adultery, have a spirit of lust, or murdered someone. God is looking to connect with you, and to blood wash you in the blood of the Lamb. Let's jump into the next example.

Acts 3:1-8 (NIV) says, "One day Peter and John were going up to the temple at the time of prayer at three in the afternoon. Now a man who was lame from birth was being carried to the temple gate called Beautiful, where he was put every day to beg from those going into the temple courts. When he saw Peter and John about to enter, he asked them for money. Peter looked straight at him, as did John. Then Peter said, "Look at us!" So, the man gave them his attention, expecting to get something from them. Then Peter said, "Silver or gold I do not have, but what I do have I give you. In the name of Jesus Christ of Nazareth, walk." Taking him by the right hand, he helped him up, and instantly the man's feet and ankles became strong. He jumped to his feet and began to walk."

Take this man who is in a destitute situation. He was begging, and he could not walk. The power of God is so strong that God does not even have to be in the room for you to have an authentic connection with Him. You must let your spirit be willing to receive the word of knowledge and the prophetic declaration into your life. Run with power. Peter spoke a prophetic or life-changing word into the man's life. It was up to the man whether he was going to make a connection with the word and put some action behind it. There were many seasons in my life where I had great men and women of God come into my life to speak a word. But I never took the word and put action behind it. I settled and stayed in my situation. If I acted, then I would be a lot further than I am now. But I thank God for the process and that God was understanding with me even when I was disobedient. Lastly, lets us look at John 5:1-15 (NIV).

"Sometime later, Jesus went up to Jerusalem for one of the Jewish festivals. Now there is in

Jerusalem near the Sheep Gate a pool, which in Aramaic is called Bethesda and which is surrounded by five covered colonnades. Here a great number of disabled people used to lie the blind, the lame, the paralyzed. One who was there had been an invalid for thirty-eight years. When Jesus saw him lying there and learned that he had been in this condition for a long time, he asked him, "Do you want to get well?" "Sir," the invalid replied, "I have no one to help me into the pool when the water is stirred. While I am trying to get in, someone else goes down ahead of me." Then Jesus said to him, "Get up! Pick up your mat and walk." At once the man was cured; he picked up his mat and walked. The day on which this took place was a Sabbath, and so the Jewish leaders said to the man who had been healed, "It is the Sabbath; the law forbids you to carry your mat." But he replied, "The man who made me well said to me, 'Pick up your mat and walk.'" So, they asked him, "Who is this fellow who told you to pick it up and walk?" The man who was healed had no idea who it was, for Jesus had slipped away into the crowd that was there. Later Jesus found him at the temple and said to him, "See, you are well again. Stop sinning or something worse may happen to you." The man went away and told the Jewish leaders that it was Jesus who had made him well."

This man was waiting at the door of his breakthrough, but he got tired and worn down. He was content sitting, waiting, and imagining what may be in the beyond for him, as many of us do. Instead of getting to a point where we are leaning and depending on our connection with God, we tend to lean on what's comfortable. "God, I know I am not supposed to be with him. He is not my purposeful spouse, God, that You have designed for me; yet, I stay. God, I know I am not supposed to fornicate, but at the moment it feels like a good thing; yet, I don't stop. God, I know I am not supposed to be attracted to the same sex, but my flesh desires it so greatly; yet, I become content. God, I know You have called me to be a Royal Priesthood and a unique generation; yet, I sell all my inheritance like the Prodigal Son. I sell my body off like a cheap piece of silver both physically and mentally." Out of all this, God says to us like the lame man at the pool of Bethesda, "Take up your bed and walk," which means grab your issues, problems, shortcomings, and past

The Plug

and follow Me. God is not concerned about our baggage. He is concerned with the contents of our heart and our willingness to make a commitment to Him and stick with it.

It's time for us to live for 'Purpose on Purpose.' Let's not discuss what we should have done and could have done. Let's start to put some action behind the words that we say out of our mouths. Death and life lies in the power of the tongue. So, let's speak life over ourselves daily with positive affirmation to build ourselves up. I will leave this closing prayer and challenge with you. The challenge is being able to connect to God by speaking to Him daily. Get in God's Word to learn more about Him. Apply this to our daily lives and **LIVE INSPIRED* DREAM INSPIRED * BE INSPIRED. *** Allow a Scripture, work, or a song to inspire you to perfect your connection with God daily.

Prayer: Father God, I thank You for allowing me to see myself through Your Word. Lord, God, I come to You right now repenting of all my sins. Lord, I come asking for guidance and protection. Teach me how to seek after You. Even when life rolls in heavy on me, teach me how to place You at the center of my life so I don't become weighed down by anxiety, depression, fear, and shame. Lord, allow me to walk in my 'Purpose on Purpose!' Lord, I pray that You strengthen my connection with You through my daily prayers, studying of Your Word and fasting. Lord, teach me how to be a true disciple of Your Word, and a great example to someone else in the body of Christ. Lord, I ask that You teach me how to love myself as You love me daily. In all these things, I ask in Jesus' name AMEN!

About the Author

Spring was born on July 4, 1989, and got her start in ministry from her grandfather/mentor, the Late Rev. Levi Gay of Gospel Mission Baptist Church of "Bridgeport, CT." Spring is an author, and Entrepreneur of Youthfullyinspired4Real Global Youth Ministries. Spring has just Blossomed into this new dimension in God. Spring Taft is a natural born leader who has a pure heart, and her only objective is to lead people to the Kingdom of God.

At a very early age, she displayed her very unique leadership skills in the kingdom of God by using her creativity to draw more young people like herself to worship and praise God authentically. Hence, "Angels of Mercies Praise Dance Team," was formed. Spring, really got ignited on her 13th birthday when she attended a Young conference in Houston, Texas at Second New Light were the Senior Pastors where Bishop IV Hillard and Pastor Brigette Hillard. Spring, was the youngest one to attend this conference out of the peers from the church. At the conference, one of the older youth and Spring felt the move of God and decided to dedicate their lives back to God. Spring has not only accomplished many things spiritually, but she is accomplishing things physically as well.

"Live on Purpose, For Purpose." Spring's future career goals are to open up her own direct care business where she is meeting the needs of others by providing them with life skills, love, appreciation, and discipleship. Also, she is looking to open up a few Youth homes (Daughters of Leah House) and (House of David). In these homes, she provides these young people with the necessary life skills with a spiritual component to help them become successful in their lives. Spring's lifetime goal is to open up a School, K-12 called the "New Remnant Academy." Spring 's purpose in life is to be the impact this world needs in whatever compacity that is.

Index

A

abandonment, 69

anchor, 19–20, 108

anointing, 44, 71

B

baggage, 68, 119

basket, 13, 16

believers, 20, 110

blessings, 15, 35, 39, 44, 56, 73–74

blood, 14, 47, 110–11, 115

blood wash, 115

brakes, 57–58

business, 79

C

capabilities, 81

chains, 113

change, 27, 50, 67, 74, 112

company, 35, 77–78

confirmation, 88

connection, 60–61, 63, 70, 90, 107–8, 110–12, 116, 118–20

conversation, 7, 9, 41, 102–3

couple, 42, 55, 94

crime, 47, 84

crowd, 1–2, 111, 117

D

daughter, 37–39, 42, 47, 79, 86–90, 94, 122

demons, 48, 113–14

departments, 35, 78, 100

destination, 98

destiny, 74, 82, 87, 91, 94

devil, 15, 42, 96

direction, 74, 91

discipleship, 122

disconnect, 60, 69

distractions, 104

distressing, 32

doctors, 14, 54

domestic violence (DV), 58, 60, 62, 64

E

earth, 31, 69, 97

earthly vessel, 103

emotions, 39, 70–72, 81, 102–3, 110

enemy, 63, 65, 71, 74, 100

excitement, 6, 21, 29

F

faith, 21, 33, 60, 91–92, 94

family, 5–6, 10, 22, 30–31, 33, 39, 43, 45, 47, 50, 60, 73–74, 78, 103

fasting, 95, 120

felony, 83–84

fight, 11, 47, 50, 57

forgive, 73–74

G

generational curses, 73

gifts, 13, 39, 74

glory, 66, 104, 115

godmother, 2, 5, 7–8, 11–13, 19, 21–29, 31

grandmother, 14, 41, 43, 45, 47, 91, 102–3

guidance, 49, 79, 119

guilt, 69, 74

H

happiness, 9, 63, 77

health, 66, 107

heart, 2, 10, 15–16, 59, 72–73, 78, 81, 96, 102, 105, 119, 121 heaviness, 68–69

Holy Spirit, 43

homeless, 35, 37, 41

honors, 5, 11, 18

house, 4, 9–11, 15, 22, 39–42, 46, 50, 55–56, 58, 81–82, 84, 91, 93, 95, 97

I

island, 60

J

Jazzy, 79–81

Jesus, 9, 24, 49, 74, 100, 110–18

K

kingdom, 15, 66, 102, 104, 121

knowledge, 62, 91, 97, 116

L

life, 1–4, 6–7, 15, 37, 39–40, 51–53, 60–63, 66–70, 73–78, 81–83, 86–89, 91–92, 104–6, 116, 119–20

life skills, 122

Lord, 2, 26, 31, 34, 73, 79, 81, 91, 94, 96, 98–99, 103, 105, 108, 119–20

M

melody, 83, 89

mind, 7, 12, 61, 69, 73–74, 85

ministry purposes, 93

misfortunes, 3, 110

money, 6, 8–10, 13, 16, 25–26, 28, 30, 35, 44, 50, 62–63, 115

O

obedience, 44, 105

P

pain, 21, 25, 30, 33–34, 37, 69–70, 72, 74, 109

peace, 51, 59, 102, 106, 108

plug-in, 108–9

porch, 22, 31, 84

position, 16, 40, 100–101, 110

power, 16, 44, 108, 116, 119

praise, 15, 20–21, 24, 27, 87, 100

pray, 13, 42, 73, 81, 92, 96–97, 120

prayer, 2, 31, 33, 44, 49, 73, 88, 115, 119

praying, 11, 33, 37, 48, 61, 68, 88, 92

promise, 7, 38, 109

prophetic, 56, 116

purification, 109

R

rain, 37

rehearsal, 8, 12, 29

relationship, 60, 68, 70, 74, 77, 90, 110, 112

S

season, 17, 32, 60, 72, 75, 77, 92, 97, 100, 102, 104, 108–9, 116

seizures, 38, 54

sex, 72, 118

shame, 69, 72, 114, 120

shock, 17, 23, 35, 64

sins, 73–74, 119

sound, 2, 40, 76

speaker, 56, 98

strength, 2, 56, 108

stress, 20, 38, 54

T

time, 2, 4–10, 15–16, 33–34, 37–38, 40, 43–45, 52, 62–66, 68–72, 79, 91–92, 94–95, 102–3, 105

touch, 48, 72, 102, 111–12

tragedy, 3

transitioning, 100

trust, 2, 92, 98, 104, 109

V

visions, 1, 63, 95, 106–7

voice, 2, 21, 61, 70, 93, 113

W

weaknesses, 108

worship, 11, 20–21, 27, 48, 87, 93, 104, 121

Y

youth, 24, 122

www.ingramcontent.com/pod-product-compliance
Lightning Source LLC
Chambersburg PA
CBHW052147110526
44591CB00012B/1884